Eat, Play, Sleep

THE ESSENTIAL GUIDE TO YOUR BABY'S FIRST THREE MONTHS

Luiza DeSouza

FOREWORD BY CINDY CRAWFORD

ATRIA BOOKS

NEW YORK   LONDON   TORONTO   SYDNEY   NEW DELHI

ATRIA BOOKS
A Division of Simon & Schuster, Inc.
1230 Avenue of the Americas
New York, NY 10020

First Atria Books hardcover edition February 2015

ATRIA B O O K S and colophon are trademarks of Simon & Schuster, Inc.

For information about special discounts for bulk purchases, please contact Simon & Schuster Special Sales at 1-866-506-1949 or business@simonandschuster.com.

The Simon & Schuster Speakers Bureau can bring authors to your live event. For more information or to book an event, contact the Simon & Schuster Speakers Bureau at 1-866-248-3049 or visit our website at www.simonspeakers.com.

Interior design by Kyoko Watanabe
Cover design by Connie Gabbert Design and Illustration

Manufactured in the United States of America

10   9   8   7   6   5   4   3   2   1

Library of Congress Cataloging-in-Publication Data is available.

ISBN 978-1-4516-5092-1
ISBN 978-1-4516-5093-8 (ebook)

This book is dedicated to Dani Michelle Jaffe,
a beautiful little girl with stars in her eyes and magic
in her heart. Dani is one of my beloved children.

All she has asked in return is that someone
consistently and sincerely love and accept her
for the unique and wonderful person that she is,
and for the magnificent woman she became.

May Dani, and all of the other children in the world,
enjoy the love, care, and respect that they deserve.

Contents

PHASE II

The First Ten Days: There's a Baby in the House!

PHASE III

The First Month: OMG, the Baby's Staying!

PHASE IV

The Second Month:
Are We Having Fun?

PHASE V

The Third Month and Beyond: Settling In and Looking Ahead

Foreword

I could not be more honored to write this Foreword for my friend Luiza DeSouza's book. Her expertise with newborns helped us enjoy every minute of early parenthood.

As a first-time mother, I didn't want anyone to interfere with my relationship with my new baby. Luiza's presence had the exact opposite effect. She helped us to bond with our son and showed us how to develop his eye contact and to encourage attachment. Also, her experience with the basics, such as bathing, swaddling, tending to the umbilical cord, and so many other little tasks of baby care, helped to create a sense of serenity around our home that most certainly rubbed off on our son. We were able to avoid that "nervous new parents" stereotype and enjoy our changed roles.

We were thrilled that Luiza was able to be with us for our second child as well. Once again, her reassuring presence enabled the three of us to smoothly transition to a family of four. Our daughter still sings her favorite Luiza lullaby, "*Cai Cai Balloon!*"

I am so glad that Luiza has taken the time to write down what she knows. She has created a book that can help parents everywhere have more confidence in caring for their babies.

Eat, Play, Sleep will answer most, if not all, of your questions, alleviate your fears, and eliminate your doubts about caring for your newborn.

Well done, Luiza!

—*Cindy Crawford*
Model, film and television actress, and mother of two
Malibu, California

Introduction

BABY NURSE TO THE RESCUE!

For thirty years I've been holding mothers' hands. I've helped women like you give their newborns the best possible start. No matter how excited you are about starting a family, no matter how prepared you think you are, it's a new role that requires a lot of education, practice, and support. I've never met a new mom who doesn't need at least a little boost of encouragement. As a professional who takes care of babies, I can show you the ropes, which will help make your life a lot happier and more peaceful. As I tell my clients, I'm here for your baby, *and* I'm here for you.

It's hard for most first-time mothers to know what to do. They're caught between their own self-doubts and the conflicting opinions of others. One of my clients told me, "I don't think I have postpartum depression, Luiza. I have postpartum *confusion!*" She knew how to be a wife and a daughter but had no idea how to be a mother.

Books can help, but if you're new to the role, you still have to figure out what ideas and techniques are right for you. The way I see it, my job is to help you sift through all the parenting advice that's thrown at you by your mother, your sister, your friends, and all those "experts" who tell you what you *must* do. I'm an expert, too, but my approach is to advise you to take your time, trust your own instincts, and choose a course that fits *your* needs and your baby's personality.

Let me take your hand. Let me be your backup. Let me show you what to look for and what to expect. Let me help you build confidence in your choices. It's not easy to be a mother. There's no magic. It's day-by-day hard work, but I *can* help.

Even if this is your second baby, he's probably nothing like your first. (My apologies if you're the mother of a girl. From this point on, you'll see that I try to alternate "he" and "she.") My advantage is that I come with three decades' worth of babies in my head and in my heart. My goal here is to peek over your shoulder and whisper encouragement into your ear. I can do for you what I've done for the mothers I've worked with over the years: help ease you into what is the most important role you'll ever play.

My Attitude Toward Childcare

Being a mother is also one of the most challenging roles you'll ever play. It's more difficult for some than for others, because of who they are, because of what kind of baby they have, and because of their life circumstances. I hope you're reading this while you're pregnant, but even if you have been home from the hospital for a week or two, you might already feel unsure of yourself. *Can I really do this?* Maybe you saw a program on TV, read a book, or took notes when your pediatrician made suggestions, and now you're afraid you can't do what "they" advise. Or perhaps you don't agree with them, because their advice doesn't suit your style. But instead of rejecting the ideas and moving on, you wonder, *Should I be doing something different, something more, for my baby?*

"Mothering" is not about programs or learning a "technique."

There is no right and wrong. Rather, mothering is about connection and relationship and getting to know who your child is. And for that reason, I believe that attitude is actually more important than approach.

When I take care of babies, I don't have a formula in my head. How could I? No two mothers are alike, and no two babies are the same. I never know what I'm going to have to deal with. Take Roberta, for example. She had a very hard time. For the first few days, Ryan had trouble latching on. Roberta's nipples were sore and cracked. Every feeding was very painful. I've seen other women give up on breast-feeding for less reason. I showed Roberta how to use breast milk on her nipples to help heal them. I told her to soak in the tub. Two years later, the two of us reminisced about my stay with her family. "It's not what you said that calmed me down, Luiza, or even what you did," she said. "It was your energy."

At first, I didn't know what she meant. I was just being me, offering her the benefit of my experience, and reassuring her that "we" would get through this. After all, I'd calmed many new mothers before, helped many babies who had trouble latching on. Thinking about it later, though, I understood that she was talking about my attitude.

In this book, I'm not going to teach you an "approach" or a structured "program." Instead, I will teach you how to *think* like me. The babies I care for thrive because I bring three important qualities into my work that influence everything I do and say: patience, openness, and attentiveness.

Patience. An expression in my native country, *Vamos devagar ate acertar*, translates roughly into, "The way to do things is little by little . . . until we get them right." Caring for a baby sometimes involves trial and error and always requires a lot of practice. To know your baby, you have to spend time with him. This isn't easy for any new mother. So take a deep breath. At some point, caring for your baby will seem easier, but this won't happen overnight. Some days will seem so long. But try to remember, *Amanha sera outro dia* ("Tomorrow is another day").

Openness. When you care for your newborn, be open to new experiences and information. I will teach you everything I have learned about caring for a newborn from the day she comes home from the hospital. I'll help you be curious and alert to what's going on in your life and in the household. Babies are very sensitive creatures; they absorb more than we realize. You are your baby's first and most important teacher. But I also urge you to open yourself to what your baby can teach *you.* Have a sense of adventure and imagination. Every day can—and probably will—bring something different. Being open will not only help you learn more about your baby, but it will also help you learn more about yourself.

Attentiveness. Many of my clients are shocked by how calm I am. In part, it's because I've been caring for newborns for so long. For example, I know for a fact that your baby won't always cry this much, and that eventually she *will* sleep through the night. I also know that when you've gotten past one hurdle, another challenge is around the corner. It's important, then, both to enjoy the moment and to look ahead and try to anticipate what's coming. You do this by watching and keeping track of your baby's progress and observing how she acts and reacts to the world. You do it by planning ahead and by not encouraging behaviors you'll have to change later and being aware of the consequences if you do. For instance, if you rock your baby every night, he learns to fall asleep that way. When he gets too heavy or you are too tired, you're in for a lot of crying when you suddenly try to change that habit. As Brazilians say, *Mais vale prevenir do que remediar* ("It's better to prevent than to have to fix").

No matter what challenges your newborn brings, patience, openness, and attentiveness will help you rise to meet them. I have seen many confused, anxious, inexperienced women become competent and, more important, confident mothers. Success builds success. The more you *feel* that you can handle it, the better you become at handling it.

When I first enter a household, I always stress that I'm there for the baby—he can't speak, so I'm his voice. But I am also very sensitive to the mother's needs. That's why much of the material in this book is designed to teach you how to care for yourself along with your baby. There is no greater gift that I can give a family than a mother who is calm, who trusts her own instincts, and who uses common sense to make adjustments along the way.

Oh, and in case you forget what I said earlier, it's not easy. There's no magic. The babies in my care do well because I put in a lot of time with them. I keep track, and I pay attention. It's hard work, day after day, and it's most challenging in the first three months. But the end result is worth working for.

My Journey: Why I Know So Much About Babies

By the time I was twenty, I was caring for infants professionally. Even though I never thought about becoming a baby nurse when I was growing up in São Paulo, when I look back now I realize I've trained my whole life to be a baby nurse. My mother, Mae, was my first teacher. Mae didn't go to school, but she was wise, honest, and a very hard worker. She took care of us seven children, cooked, cleaned, and still made time to help others.

One of my earliest memories is of our small living room filled with mothers sitting with their babies. We lived in a poor neighborhood, where most women couldn't afford to see a doctor, so they came to our house instead. Mae had a gift. She was a healer. She would take the crying infant onto her lap, massage his back, gently straighten out one leg and then the other. Sometimes she would put her hands on the baby's forehead, letting the heat of her hands calm him. She would talk softly. I knew she was praying for God to ease that baby's pain.

As the oldest child in the family, I was very close to my mother. I became strong and confident because Mae treated me like an adult from a very early age. When I was only five or six, she began to teach me how to cook, clean, and care for children—everything she did. There was always a new baby in our house, even after we moved to Campinas, a small town an hour and a half away, so that my father could take a better job in a bakery. I was twelve then; five years later, my youngest brother was born.

I had cared for many of my younger siblings, but Francisco was like *my* baby. When I was seventeen, although I knew I'd miss him desperately, I wanted to begin making my own way in the world. I also wanted to help my family. I didn't know how, but life has a funny way of presenting opportunities if you're ready for them.

Shortly after I turned eighteen, I went back to São Paulo to pay a visit to my cousin, who was then working as a nurse at the very well-respected Beneficência Portuguesa (Charity Hospital of Portugal). She thought I'd be perfect for the new two-year training program for assistant nurses. As a trainee, I would work in exchange for room and board and tuition. I enrolled immediately.

After six months in the program, rotating from one section to another, I was assigned to the maternity ward of the hospital. I fell in love with the newborns. Being there didn't feel like work. The babies were tiny and helpless, struggling to adjust to life outside the womb. The nun who supervised the ward, Lucia, saw my passion and became my mentor. When a paid position opened in the maternity ward, she asked if I'd be willing to drop out of the training program and work full-time. It meant I'd finally earn money, so of course, I said yes.

I worked on the ward for more than a year, dealing only with newborns. I wore a starched white uniform and white shoes, a hairnet and a little pointed nurse's hat on my head. There were six or seven nurses per shift. Each of us was assigned to several babies, depending on how full the ward was. On a typical eight-hour shift, I had three or four newborns under my care, but when the moon was full—a time when babies tend to be born—I'd have as many as six or seven. We also took turns, once a week, in the *lactario*, where formula was prepared.

In those days, we boiled everything—nipples, bottles, water. Babies never slept in their mothers' rooms as they sometimes do now. Babies were in nurses' care—that was the rule. We'd take the little ones to their mothers every four hours, like clockwork, and then take them away. We also weighed the babies before and after nursing. If a baby hadn't gained weight after a feeding, we suspected that she wasn't getting enough breast milk, so we'd give her formula, too. In between feedings, we also gave the babies sugar water to keep them from becoming dehydrated. Today, of course, newborns are not kept on rigid schedules, and they're never given water at such an early age.

To make extra money on my days off, I started working as a health aide, helping new mothers. I learned that some rich families in Brazil hired private baby nurses to help take care of their newborns for several weeks, even months. I asked Lucia, "How can I do that?"

A few months later, Lucia recommended me to a doctor whose wife had just had their third child. One of the older children had a contagious virus, and the couple decided that the newborn should stay in the city with his maternal grandmother. The baby's mother and siblings would go to the family's beach house.

When the doctor brought me to the grandmother's very fancy apartment, she took one look at me and said to him, "Are you really going to leave your son in the hands of this *kid*?"

I can't blame her. I was nineteen but looked more like a fifteen-year-old. The doctor stuck up for me, though, because Lucia had recommended me so highly. "She's not a kid," he responded. "And she knows what she's doing."

I was hired for one month but ended up being with that family for nearly three. My next job was with friends of the doctor, and word spread quickly after that. I had the advantage of not being German, like most of the private baby nurses in Brazil in the mid-1960s. The German baby nurses were very strict and old-fashioned. Some didn't even let mothers come into the nursery. I was different—much more relaxed, softer. I took care of the baby, but I also wanted the mother involved. I knew how important it was for mothers to bond with their babies.

Eventually, I became the number one baby nurse in São Paulo. Despite my being so young, the mothers I worked for trusted me. For a "kid," I knew a lot, sometimes more than I realized myself. A particular scene stands out in my mind. My boyfriend Fernando and I had decided to spend the weekend in Salto de Itu, a small town on the outskirts of São Paulo. He was at the university studying sociology at the time, and I had a few days off. We stayed in a small family-run hotel. Our first night there, the sound of a screaming baby pierced the air. "Waa . . . waaa . . . waa . . ." Everyone knows what an upsetting noise that is, especially when you're trying to fall asleep. I could tell from the cries that it was a newborn. Finally, I couldn't take it any longer, so I left our room and knocked on the door of the main house. There, looking exhausted, were Grandma and Grandpa, in their forties, and the young parents, who were probably around my age. "I'm Luiza. I'm a baby nurse," I explained. "Can I help?"

The grandmother hesitated only a moment before she gave me the baby. Recalling that incident, I think about how brave I was at twenty-two. No one would do that today. Knock on a total stranger's door? The family told me that they had fed the baby several times and given him chamomile tea in case he had a tummyache. But nothing they did seemed to help. With their permission, I swaddled the baby and held him in an upright position on my chest. In minutes, he calmed down and, just like an angel, fell asleep.

The four of them looked at me, amazed. But what I had done wasn't extraordinary. I just knew how to hold the baby to relieve his distress. I also realized that the baby was so overtired from crying that he couldn't fall asleep without help. By swaddling him, I prevented his body from moving. Keeping him in an upright position close to my beating heart helped him to calm down and fall asleep.

When I came back to our room and told Fernando what had happened, he said, "Luiza, you know you have a gift, don't you?"

My confidence then—as now—came, first, from my mother. The years I spent watching and helping Mae gave me good instincts. She trusted me with my younger siblings, so I trusted myself. My time at Beneficência Portuguesa, caring for several newborns at once—often under great pressure—gave me skills. Because I was so hungry to learn and to better myself, I was open to new ideas. I paid close attention to the more experienced nurses, the pediatricians, and the lactation consultants I worked with at the hospital. When I left Brazil to become a baby nurse in the United States, I studied child development and worked in special education in the San Diego schools, with children who, like infants, required sensitivity and patience. Today, when a client asks, as many do, "Luiza, how did you learn this?" I can see how one step led to the next. I also know that most of my confidence comes from positive results. Babies thrive in my care.

I often think of my mother when I have a crying baby who is hard to soothe. I go to a quiet place with the baby and hold her close to my heart. Sometimes I massage her the way my mother did. Or I just place my hands close to the baby's body or forehead, letting my hands comfort her as my mother did when I was a child and had a fever or pain. And sometimes I use my thoughts to calm the baby—not prayers the way Mae did but a kind of silent reassurance. My boyfriend Fernando was right: I do have a gift. But we all can have this gift—if we learn how to use it. In this book, I'll teach you how.

I will give you the benefit of all my experience and teach you how to think like me. I will help you become more patient, open, and attentive, just as I have learned in the course of my long career. And in the end, you, too, will trust yourself. Of course, you'll be tired and frustrated at times—that goes with the territory. You'll work hard. I certainly do! But little by little, you will also keep getting better at your "job," which will not only make you proud but will also give you the confidence to trust your instincts and to know that you can handle whatever comes your way. A careful beginning will not only benefit your baby's emotional and social development, but it will give you a good start, too.

Mom, I'm Here for *You*

Whether you are the biological or the adoptive mother, *you* are the person I'm talking to. You protect your infant and make sense of the world for him. You introduce him to his environment and help him adapt. Others love him and care for him, I'm sure, but at this stage of your baby's development, you are the most important person in his life.

My intention isn't to insult or exclude anyone by assuming that a woman is usually the primary caretaker. I have seen many fathers who are willing to change diapers and others who get up in the middle of the night to comfort a sick child. But I know from experience that unless there is no woman in the household, during the first three months of a baby's life, the mother does most of the work.

Maybe your husband announced to family and friends, "We

are pregnant." Many a young father-to-be nowadays refers to his wife's pregnancy as if it's his, too. The baby is, that's for sure. But it is *your* body that carried the baby and changed as a result. *You* endured the pain, nausea, and extra weight. Although the baby belongs to both of you, it's your life that will change most dramatically, especially over these early months. You will be the first to bond with your baby.

I recognize, of course, that modern families are not necessarily headed by a man and a woman. Some gay men and lesbians create families through adoption. Male couples also become fathers through surrogacy; lesbians use sperm donors. But I've observed that also in these households, one parent is more hands-on than the other. One is more comfortable with baby care, and the other—usually the breadwinner—has less time to devote to the newborn.

Of course, no matter whom you partner with, if there's a new baby in your household and you're the primary caretaker, you know it! If you're reading this book and you are a male caretaker—straight or gay—when I say "mom" and "mother," I'm talking to you, too.

If being the One feels like a big responsibility, it is. But you don't have to handle it on your own. Ideally, your partner is eager to pitch in with the baby and also willing to nurture *you*. You might also have a loving family and friends who can make these early (sleepless and confusing) months a little easier. But regardless of your situation, let me now take you by the hand. Allow me to help you and support you in this difficult task.

How to Use This Book

In these pages, I offer you everything I've learned, everything you need to know about taking care of your baby. Believe me, I know how overwhelming it is to have a new baby. It's unfamiliar territory. How can it not feel scary at times? But as your baby grows, I promise, so will your knowledge.

To simplify, I present information here the way I do with my clients: on a need-to-know basis. In other words, I've sorted the advice according to how and when it usually comes up when I take care of a baby. For example, you need to know about swaddling immediately—it helps your newborn sleep—but you shouldn't be thinking about your baby sleeping through the night until she's at least two months old. The book is therefore divided into short, manageable phases. The first chapter is about "Getting Ready and Set," the preparation phase. If you're reading this book while you are pregnant, "What You Need Before" will help you figure out what to have on hand and how to organize it. (If you're all set, it can be helpful to read chapter 1 anyway, just to make sure you haven't forgotten anything.) Four other phases complete the book:

- The First Ten Days
- The First Month
- The Second Month
- The Third Month and Beyond

Each of these phases contains several chapters that cover topics you can expect to encounter or should think about during that phase. Each opens with an introduction to the key challenges of that phase—and a list of chapter topics "In a Nutshell," followed by a few paragraphs that will give you an overall sense of what to expect.

I've tried to design the book to make it easy for you to follow and to find things when you need them. Various boxes and sidebars with additional information are scattered throughout, such as the "What If . . ." sections that deal with commonly encountered problems.

Read along, day by day, as your baby grows and you experience new motherhood. Remember, though, that your baby is unique; she'll develop at her own rate. Thus, each phase in this book is meant as a rough guideline. For example, although phase II is devoted to the first ten days, it actually covers, more or less, the first seven to twelve days. It depends on your baby's weight, how your delivery went, and whether either of you has any health problems.

Let's say that your first-days-of-motherhood story is something like my old client Roberta's. Your baby is small at birth, he has trouble latching on when you try to breast-feed, and, as a result, he's still struggling to gain weight. Your nipples are raw and painful. Even though you are chronologically almost into your third week of new motherhood, you might still be dealing with issues that typically resolve themselves in the first week.

Also, many factors work together to determine what your homecoming will be like—who's in your household, what kind of help you have, whether and how soon you'll be going back to work. When material covered in an earlier phase comes up later in the book, you'll find a cross-reference in case you need to go back, reread, and refresh your memory. You can also use the index to look up a topic.

Most important, at the end of each phase, I've provided a page for notes. I can't emphasize enough how important it is for you to keep track. This will help you practically; in the haze of early motherhood, it's easy to forget something that happened a few days earlier. And it will also help you emotionally, by giving you perspective. You can see how far you've come.

I've done my best to make the book clear and usable. I hope you'll do your best to be open, patient, and attentive and to allow me to help you. We can work as a team to welcome and nurture this tiny, miraculous creature who's come into your life. From this point forward, let's pretend that we are reading this book together.

PHASE I

The Weeks Before "Go": Getting Ready and Set

Chapter 1

WHAT YOU NEED BEFORE

Once a family decides to hire me—which usually happens early in the woman's pregnancy—I pay a visit a few weeks before the due date. I help her think about what she needs to pack before she goes to the hospital (see sidebar). I also want to help her arrange the nursery and go over a checklist of items she'll need to have when she comes home from the hospital. Some families are superstitious, feeling that something might go wrong if they buy clothing and equipment before the baby is actually here. I can respect that, but I also know that if the necessities are there—organized and ready for you to use—you'll have a much easier transition from hospital to home.

Some parents have an abundance of "baby things"—equipment, toys, clothing—that they've received from excited relatives and friends. Others become anxious about not having enough or having the "right" things, so they buy too much. First-timers often think they have to get *everything*—and get it *right away.* You don't. You're thinking too far ahead. At this point, all you have to do is purchase what you need for the next three months—and it's probably less than you think.

WHAT TO PACK WHEN YOU'RE EXPECTING

The first step of good preparation for motherhood is your hospital bag. However long you stay—usually two days if there are no complications—and if the hospital supplies clothing for your baby (call the maternity ward to check), you don't need much.

For you

* Lip balm (lips get dry during labor)
* Hair band (if you have long hair, you'll probably want it tied up during labor)
* Underwear, 3 pairs
* Sanitary pads (hospitals supply these, but if you have a favorite brand, bring a box)
* Pajamas, 2 pairs
* Robe
* Slippers
* Toiletries (shampoo, conditioner, soap, toothbrush, toothpaste)
* Notebook and pen
* Books, magazines
* Phone, tablet, other gadgets (optional)

For the baby

In most hospitals, babies are dressed in a long-sleeved white shirt and swaddled in a thin flannel blanket. If you prefer to bring your own clothes and hospital policy permits, take two or three extra outfits for the stay. For the trip home, pack a warm blanket, a hat, and another simple outfit. If it's winter, pack extra layers to protect him from the cold.

Some things you can borrow, and some things you can buy used or at great discounts. If your budget is tight, read on, and make a list of what you really need. Start early, so you can take your time finding good stores or websites. Everything you buy, though, should meet current government safety standards. Most of your questions can be answered by the Consumer Product Safety Commission, toll-free at (800) 638-2772 or online at: https://www.cpsc.gov. Another useful resource is *Consumer Reports*, which tests, rates, and compares products, at http://www.consumerreports.org.

Used or new, you certainly don't need a lot of equipment, supplies, or clothing when you come home from the hospital. But you will need to make six preliminary decisions that will affect what you need. The questions below will help you gauge what you need for your baby and yourself when the baby is born and during the next three months. The earlier you answer them, the better prepared you'll feel. You'll be able to focus on your baby and your experiences as a new mother, without having to scramble at the last minute. At least in the practical sense, you'll be prepared.

1. How will I take my baby home and, later, on outings?
2. How will I feed my baby?
3. How and where will I dress and bathe my baby?
4. Will I use cloth or disposable diapers?
5. Where will my baby sleep?
6. How will I soothe, amuse, and protect my baby?

I'll help you think about these questions in the sections below. To make it easier to scan this chapter, for each section, you'll find a list of the items you need to buy or borrow depending on your answer. If you already have everything on hand, it doesn't hurt to skim this chapter and double-check.

1. How Will I Take My Baby Home and, Later, on Outings?

If you have to drive home from the hospital—as most parents do—you'll need a car seat. Most seats snap out and double as a baby carrier, a little seat in which your baby can recline. Be sure that the car seat is installed properly. If necessary, ask another parent or go to your local police or fire department for help.

GETTING AROUND

* Car seat
* Carriage or stroller
* Kangaroo-type carrier
* Baby carrier

For outings, you'll also want a carriage or stroller. Many models double as both. Most are collapsible and have seats that can be adjusted as your baby grows. Assuming your baby is eight pounds or more, sometime during the first month, you can also take walks with your baby using a kangaroo-type carrier that's worn on the front of your chest. (Back carriers shouldn't be used with newborns.) But first, check with your pediatrician, and read the instructions before your first outing. Kangaroo carriers are also handy for comforting your new baby.

2. How Will I Feed My Baby?

Breast milk or formula? That's one of the first questions I ask a prospective client, because the answer tells me what kind of equipment she'll need. Today almost everyone recommends breast-feeding—it's "in fashion." Most women at least consider it. Babies who are born full-term and weigh six to eight pounds at birth normally have no problem nursing. Even though breast-feeding can feel like a challenge during the first few days, it's the easiest way to feed a baby. It's also the more economical choice. The most popular formulas are not too costly, but if your baby's digestive system doesn't tolerate them, you might have to buy a more expensive alternative.

Convenience and cost aside, however, babies who are breast-fed exclusively—no water, juice, or solids—for the first six months are better protected against many diseases, according to the American Academy of Pediatrics. By starting out with breast milk, your newborn will benefit from colostrum, the vitamin-rich, immune-boosting substance that your breasts initially produce. Colostrum is almost like a medication, because it prepares your child's digestive system. There is no substitute for it.

That said, *not every woman can, or wants to, breast-feed.* Formula—enhanced cow's milk—is a good second choice. Formula is similar to breast milk in terms of nutritional value. Formula-feeding is also a more flexible option, because you can let others care for your baby. Newborns on formula last longer between feedings than newborns on breast milk, but once breast-feeding is well established, that difference disappears. So if you haven't yet decided between the two and you are reading this while pregnant or shortly after your delivery, at least *try* to breast-feed for three or four days (I'll guide you in chapter 7).

FEEDING

* Bibs
* Burp cloths
* A few cloth diapers

For breast-feeding

* Nursing bras
* Disposable maternity pads
* Breast pump
* Bags/containers for stored breast milk
* Boppy or firm pillow

For bottle-feeding

* Baby bottles, 4- and 8-ounce size
* Silicone nipples
* Plastic protector caps
* Bottle brush

No matter what you decide, babies spit up during and after they eat. To keep your baby's chest dry and protect your own clothing, buy soft bibs and burp cloths (a cloth diaper can also serve this purpose). Below, I look at what else you'll need for each feeding regimen. You might actually need both kinds of supplies even if you decide to breast-feed. Bottles are not just for formula. Once your milk flow is established, Dad and other family members and caretakers can feed the baby breast milk in a bottle. Also, breast-feeding doesn't always go as planned. Some women change their minds. Others need to supplement with formula.

Breast-Feeding

Buy a special nursing bra. A well-made, proper-fitting bra will provide the best support and help prevent or minimize back pain. Maternity bras come in many styles, so choose one that is comfortable for your body and easy to open and close. However, only buy one bra until you know for sure that the size and style are good for your postbaby body. You might also want to buy disposable maternity pads, which are placed inside the bra to help keep your outer garments dry and unstained. This is a personal and practical decision. Some women use pads all the time, others only when wearing good clothes.

Buy or rent a breast pump. It's a necessity if you want to express milk into a bottle, which enables your partner or a baby nurse to feed the baby. A manual pump is less expensive but also more time-consuming than an electric breast pump. I usually advise mothers to rent the more powerful electric pumps. Some moms also invest in a Boppy, also called a newborn lounger. It's a big pillow designed to support the baby while nursing. Standard firm sleeping pillows work just as well. Use as many as you need to feel fully supported and comfortable.

Bottle-Feeding

When choosing baby bottles, look for those that are completely smooth inside, because they are easier to clean. Start with eight to ten four-ounce bottles that come with nipples and plastic protector caps, and get a bottle brush. After the first month, as your baby increases her intake, you'll probably need eight-ounce bottles, too. How many you buy depends on how far in advance you want to prepare them. If you plan to mix enough formula for a twenty-four-hour cycle, you'll need at least eight. But if you prepare bottles as needed, then two or three will be enough.

3. How and Where Will I Dress and Bathe My Baby?

I recommend a combination dresser and changing table with drawers for clothes and diapers underneath and, on top, a padded cover and a little space for your baby's toiletries. But if your budget is tight, you don't *need* one. Any hard, flat surface covered with foam or a few thick towels will do. A dresser-height surface will be easier on your back, so the kitchen counter is better than your bed. When I travel with clients, I usually set up a changing table on a countertop in the bathroom.

For dressing and after-bath care, have these items within easy reach: a soft-bristled hairbrush, baby nail scissors, a soft nail file, alcohol (to clean the umbilical cord), and cotton swabs.

Your baby doesn't need much clothing; just have a few basic items on hand (see box). I like to stick with white cotton fabric, because it breathes and is less likely to irritate your baby's sensitive skin.

Keep clothing simple. Your baby can live in "onesies," one-piece T-shirts that snap on the bottom to keep the shirt from

DRESSING/BATHING

- Changing table
- Hairbrush
- Baby nail scissors
- Soft nail file
- Rubbing alcohol
- Cotton swabs
- Mild, nonchemical laundry detergent
- Portable infant tub
- Hooded towels, 3 or 4
- Baby washcloths, 6
- Nonscented soap or body wash
- "Tearless" shampoo
- White onesies, 6, sizes 0–3 months and 3–6 months
- One-piece outfits with snaps from neck to toe, 6
- Kimonos for sleeping
- Snowsuit for cold weather
- Socks and mittens for the cold
- "Special occasion" outfits, 1 or 2 (you probably were given these as gifts)

riding up. They're especially good during the hot months of summer. If you buy pants or one-piece outfits, look for the kind that open from the bottom with snaps along the inseam for easier access to diapers. Avoid garments with buttons. As your precious little one becomes better coordinated, broken buttons can be picked up and swallowed. Buy a range of sizes—say, 0–3 months and 3–6 months. Save the receipts and don't remove the tags; return anything that's too small. Wash baby clothes separately with a mild, nonchemical detergent.

For bathing your baby, I recommend buying a portable baby tub that can be placed on a counter or in your bathroom tub (although this is often harder on your back). Many of the newer infant tubs feature special inserts that hold the baby in a comfortable position. Buy a tub that makes *you* comfortable, too; you want to be as relaxed as possible. Some moms bathe their babies in the kitchen sink. That's fine, as long as it's big enough for you to hold on to your baby securely. Bathroom sinks are usually too small, and the low faucets get in the way.

You'll also need baby washcloths, nonscented soap or body wash such as Cetaphil, "tearless" baby shampoo, and hooded towels to keep your little one dry and cozy afterward.

4. Will I Use Cloth or Disposable Diapers?

Modern mothers often don't even bother to ask my opinion on this. Some don't want the hassle of washing diapers or using a diaper service, so they buy disposables. Others worry about the environment. Cloth diapers can cost less than a month of disposables, but they don't necessarily have less of an impact on the environment. I'm no scientist, but I imagine that the washers and dryers used to clean cloth diapers—your own or those used by a service—leave a carbon footprint, too.

> **DIAPERING**
>
> - Wipes or cotton squares
> - Diaper cream
> - Triple antibiotic cream
> - Wipe warmer (optional)
>
> **If you use cloth**
>
> - 100% cotton diapers, 3–6 dozen
> - Container for soiled diapers
>
> **If you use disposable**
>
> - Newborn-size diapers, 1–2 packages
> - Diaper Genie or other type of diaper disposal

Whatever your decision, you'll have to clean your baby's bottom at *every* diaper change. I use premoistened hypoallergenic cotton wipes or cotton squares dipped in a small bowl of plain tap water, which you keep on the changing table. As long as you dip only *clean* squares into the bowl, you don't have to change the water after each diaper change. I also use two kinds of diaper cream: one for diaper rash prevention (I use Aquaphor at every diaper change) and, if necessary, a triple antibiotic ointment such as Triple Paste Diaper Rash Ointment for healing raw, delicate skin.

Cloth Diapers

If you plan to wash them yourself, purchase three dozen to six dozen 100-percent-cotton cloth diapers, and if you don't pay a diaper service to do it for you, wash soiled diapers in the same mild, nonchemical detergent you use for your baby's clothing. You'll also need a closed container for soiled diapers.

If you use a diaper service, order eighty to one hundred diapers a week at first. Some companies supply both the diapers and the container. If you go this route, look into it at least two months before your due date, so that you're not scrambling around at the last minute.

Disposable Diapers

To start, buy the newborn size. There's no way to guess how many diapers your baby will need at first; it depends on her birth weight and how much she eats and grows. Buy one or two packages initially and keep the receipts. Most stores will allow customers to return unopen packages. You'll also need a diaper disposal nearby, a special covered container that traps diaper odor.

5. Where Will My Baby Sleep?

Your baby can sleep in his own bed or join you in what is now thought of as the "family bed." I believe babies should have their own beds, but you have to answer this question for yourself. Co-sleeping, as it's sometimes called, requires no equipment. But even if you decide to bring your newborn into your bed, consider having another place where he can take naps or sleep at night if you or your partner are sick. Also, some parents embrace the idea of co-sleeping and then change their minds once the baby comes and they actually start doing it. Whether this happens in the first week or months later, you'll need a plan B.

For the baby's own bed, you can start with a "Moses basket," which can be carried from room to room, or a bassinet, which is bigger and sits on a stand. Both can be pushed around and are easier to lean over than a crib. These smaller alternatives to a crib are cozier for a newborn—more like being in utero—and more portable, allowing you to have the baby in whatever room you like. I generally use a bassinet for three months; once the baby starts to move, I feel that a crib is more appropriate. If you are more comfortable with your baby in a bassinet, you can extend her time there, but move her to a crib when she starts to roll over from her tummy to her back, which could happen anytime from the fourth month on.

You may not have to buy a Moses basket or a bassinet if a relative or friend has recently had a baby. Most people use them for only a short time and are happy to share. You also might find one for resale. Make sure it is clean and sturdy. Buy a firm, snug-fitting cradle mattress, and cover it with a waterproof mattress protector and sheet of the same size.

When you buy a crib for your newborn, make sure that it is adjustable, allowing the mattress to be higher in the first four months. It will be a lot easier on your back. The lower the mat-

---

SLEEPING

- Moses basket or bassinet
- Cradle-size waterproof mattress cover
- Cradle-size fitted sheets, 2
- Crib
- Crib-size waterproof mattress cover
- Fitted crib sheets, 2
- Crib bumpers
- Swaddling blankets, 4–6
- Sleep sack

tress, the more difficult it is to put the baby in, especially for short people.

Many department stores order cribs directly from the manu-facturers, which means it can take up to twelve weeks for delivery. So it's smart to buy your crib at least four months before your baby is due. This gives you plenty of time to receive your crib and set it up. If your baby surprises you and comes early, use a bassinet or a Moses basket in the meantime.

Invest in a good, tight-fitting crib mattress, a waterproof mattress protector, and at least two crib sheets that fit your par-ticular mattress. Your baby, and perhaps others in the future, will be in this crib for at least two years. Make sure the mattress itself fits snugly into the crib frame, so that there's no space around the edges. You'll also need a set of bumpers—padding that goes around the inside of the crib. When choosing bumpers, make sure they are thin and firm. Babies quickly begin to move around, and cushioned bumpers can be a breathing hazard.

Don't worry about buying blankets or a quilt for the crib. In-stead, buy four to six swaddling blankets. There are many types on the market. I like the Miracle blanket or the Bamboo Swaddle by Aden & Anais, but you can also swaddle your baby in any light cotton "receiving" blanket. Once you no longer swaddle your baby, when it's cold at night, it's better to put her in a "sleep sack," a wearable blanket that zips up the front.

6. How Will I Soothe, Amuse, and Protect My Baby?

You will use your voice to calm her, your eyes to connect, and your hands to caress. You will be your baby's whole world at first. Gradually, and with great care, you'll start to coax her to spend little bits of time on her own. Here are a few items that can help.

Soothing

Of course, you can sit in any kind of chair with your infant, but I recommend a rocker or a plushly padded chair. If you already have such a chair in your house, move it into the baby's room. When you soothe or feed him, it will make *you* more comfortable, too. A small lamp is a nice touch, because the lighting is less harsh than an overhead fixture.

Amusing

It's important to stimulate your baby, but you don't have to entertain her all the time. She can amuse herself by looking out a window or around the room. In her crib, she can gaze up at her mobile or look at colorful (store-bought or handmade) drawings you place around her crib, a hand's distance from her face. I also like to give the baby a change of scene by laying her down on a Gymini, a lightly padded floor mat that has toys dangling overhead.

To calm your baby when you're not holding him, consider buying a baby swing that you can move around the house or an infant chair that you can put on top of a table. Ask your friends and search the internet to find models you like. Both are convenient for keeping your baby close while you're in the kitchen, having a shower, or working around the house. If you have a CD

SOOTHING, AMUSING, PROTECTING

- Comfortable chair
- Small lamp
- Colorful drawings
- Mobile Gymini
- iPod or white-noise machine
- Baby swing
- Infant seat
- Baby monitor
- Bulb-type nasal aspirator

or MP3 player or can buy one, it's a great way to introduce your baby to the joy of soft music and the soothing tones of nature. Some parents also use a white-noise machine to block sounds from the household when the baby is asleep.

Protecting

It's important to leave your baby on his own for periods of time, certainly when he's sleeping but also when he's awake and happily amusing himself. A baby monitor will give you peace of mind. One warning, though: babies make all sorts of noises while they're sleeping, and not every one of them means "Mommy, come here now!" I promise you, though, if you take your time, you'll learn what all those cries and whimpers mean.

Most newborns don't get fevers or colds in the first three months, but some do. It's not necessary to keep medicines on hand until your pediatrician prescribes them. But it's important to have a thermometer and a bulb-type nasal aspirator stored away, just in case.

A Place for Everything and Everything in Its Place

Of course, you could buy more, but why? These first few months are going to fly by, and most of what you buy or borrow today will be useless in three months. The next step is to organize all your baby stuff.

Whether your baby has his own room or shares one with a sibling, knowing where things are and having them within easy reach make everyone's life easier. Start with the changing table. The diapers, the wipes, the ointment—everything you use daily— should be at arm's length. You'll be diapering ten or twelve times a day at first. For the same reason, it's also handy to position the chair you use for feeding next to a side table with a drawer or next to a set of open shelves. That way, you can have a glass of water handy, or if you suddenly need something, such as a burp cloth in case of a spit-up, it's right there for you.

Your diaper container and a hamper or laundry basket for soiled clothes should be within tossing distance of the changing table, so that you can keep your baby's clothing separate from your own.

If you live in a two-story house, set up a changing area on each floor—say, one upstairs in the baby's room or near the area where she sleeps and another on the ground floor. That way, you don't have to climb a flight of stairs each time your baby needs a new diaper. Minimize your need to keep track by having dedicated areas for baby stuff wherever possible. In the kitchen, pick a shelf to store your baby's bottles, nipples, containers, and formula. In one bathroom, set aside her medicines, have a place for her tub, and hang her robe on the back of the door. The trick is to know where everything is without even having to think about it.

Finally, your baby will start accumulating toys long before he can actually reach for them, so you might want to invest in a plastic bin. Even if you don't go overboard yourself, visitors will come bearing plush animals and shaky toys. Eventually, your baby will discover them, too.

◆ ◆ ◆

If you start with these essentials, you'll be prepared but not overstocked. Put them on your baby shower wish list. Get only what you need. And now the adventure begins. You're about to discover your individual baby's needs.

Notes on the Weeks Before "Go"

About Me/Us

_____

_____

_____

_____

_____

My Pregnancy

_____

_____

_____

_____

_____

What I/We Did to Prepare for the Baby

_____

_____

_____

_____

_____

What Was Happening in the World

_____

_____

_____

_____

_____

My Baby Shower

_____

_____

_____

_____

Other Memories of "Before"

_____

_____

_____

_____

Our Family

Looking at your extended family helps you see where your baby comes from and how many people love and support her. If your family is bigger (or more complicated) than this simple diagram allows, add more boxes and lines.

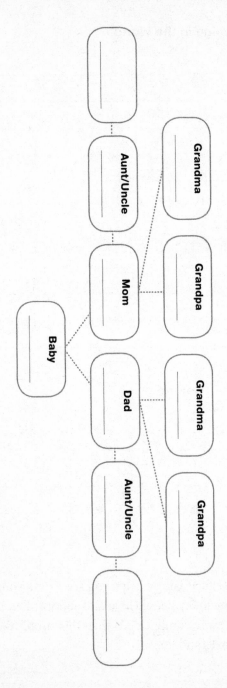

PHASE II

The First Ten Days:
There's a Baby in the House!

IN A NUTSHELL

The most important thing now is for you to rest and make sure your new baby is comfortable. He will mostly sleep, waking up for feeds, and, almost immediately, go back to sleep. When he's in his bassinet or crib, keep him swaddled in a cotton blanket. Feed him—unswaddled—whenever he wakes up during the day and night.

COVERED IN THIS PHASE:

Your newborn's looks and other surprises

Bonding with your baby

Being with your newborn

A clean start

Feeding basics

If you breast-feed

Protecting your newborn

$\mathcal{A}$lthough I often start a job by meeting the parents at the hospital, I met Lauren a few days later. When I asked how she was doing, her answer reminded me of so many of the new moms I've met over the years.

"Oh, God!" she started. "My breasts hurt, I'm gassy, and I can't go to the bathroom. I really want to be happy, Luiza, and I want to take care of my baby, but he is so tiny. I'm afraid I'll do the wrong thing. Yesterday he was hungry all the time. The lactation nurse in the hospital told me to feed him on demand, but now I'm not so sure what that means. He seems to sleep a lot. Am I supposed to wake him? I forgot to ask. But I've heard that it is not right to wake a sleeping baby. I'm so confused."

Lauren stopped for a moment to catch her breath. "I can't think clearly; I keep forgetting even familiar names," she continued. "Making everything worse, my husband is already complaining that everything is about the baby. How can he demand my attention *now*? I feel alone and exhausted. If only I could have stayed in the hospital, just one more day . . ."

No wonder Lauren had fantasies of staying in the hospital. When Max arrived, she was surrounded by knowledgeable people—doctors, nurses, a lactation specialist. But now *she* was in charge. I took Lauren's hands in mine, as I do with so many new clients. "Don't worry. Caring for your baby will be easier than you think. You already have a connection to him—you've been together for the last nine months."

When you come home with a new baby, it *is* confusing. Everyone has an opinion, even those who have no experience with infants. It's absolutely normal to feel overwhelmed. A little voice inside asks, *Are you sure you can handle this?*

Don't panic. Even I, who have been working with babies

almost my entire life, also feel a little hesitant when I first start to care for a newborn. He already has a personality, but I know almost nothing about him. So it takes me a few days, sometimes longer, to understand him. I eventually get to know him, because I remember to be patient, open, and attentive. I try one thing, then another. My goal is to create a comfortable environment for that particular baby. When I discover something that works, I stick with it. Let's take a deep breath and look at this much-awaited phase. It's a big job, because everything is new. But I'm going to break it down into small pieces. A day at a time, you *can* get through.

Make this a quiet time. You're exhausted, and your baby is not fully "here" yet. She might be sleeping off any drugs that were administered when you were in labor, or maybe she's just tired from the journey. Your most important job is to show her that the world is a welcoming place. (You should be prepared in the practical sense. If not, reread chapter 1.)

In the old days in Brazil, they called this time *quarentena*. I remember my mother making chicken soup when anyone gave birth. All the women around the new mother would take over her everyday tasks so she could rest, rest, rest. Although many modern women feel they need to "bounce back" after childbirth, it's best to give yourself time just to "nest" with your baby. Get out of bed or even out of the house if you must, but don't overdo it.

Believe me, this brief phase of motherhood will fly by.

Chapter 2

HELLO, BABY:
YOUR NEWBORN'S LOOKS AND
OTHER SURPRISES

One of my clients still teases her mother about the expression on her face when she first laid eyes on her new grandson. "I could tell you were shocked—and not in a good way." Most newborns don't look as if they belong on the cover of a baby magazine. Most parents don't imagine the squished nose, the funny-shaped head, and the swollen lips. Trust me, she'll look quite different in a week. No matter what your baby looks like, though, to you, she's probably beautiful.

Of course, the first thing you want to know is if she's "normal." Size is one factor. The average baby weighs between six and eight pounds and is between eighteen and twenty-two inches long. You've probably already counted her fingers and toes. But you also might wonder about other parts of her body and how she moves. Let me help you . . .

The Body Parts

Head

Your baby's head might look huge to you. It should. At birth, it's one-quarter of his size! He's so top-heavy he can flop back dangerously if you don't support his head and neck whenever you pick him up. The genius of nature is that the top of his head is not fully formed until *after* birth. This partially closed skull allows a baby to slither through his mother's birth canal. (If you had a cesarean section, it was probably because your baby's size or position made this impossible.)

The fontanels, or "soft spots" where your baby's skull bones are still separated, are above his brow, on his forehead and on the crown of his head. Both are covered with a thick, protective fiber layer. If you touch the soft spot on the top of his head, you can actually feel his pulse. Be careful to treat the area gently, especially at this age, when your baby is most vulnerable. Also, to avoid flat head, which can happen when an infant always sleeps in the same position, switch sides each time you lay your baby down.

Depending on the kind of delivery you had, you also might see forcep marks on the sides of the baby's head, in front of her ears, or marks left by a vacuum extractor on the back or crown of his head. If you pushed a lot during the delivery, your baby might have a lump on one side of his head. A narrow birth canal and an accumulation of liquids can also cause swelling. Your pediatrician will reassure you that these are not serious conditions. Most disappear by the time your baby is two or three months old, some in a matter of weeks.

Eyes

Dark-skinned children are generally born with chestnut-gray eyes that become darker by two months. Light-skinned newborns usually have blue-gray eyes that can take as long as five or six months to stabilize. If your baby was given silver nitrate eye drops soon after birth, her eyes might appear silver for a few days before the natural color is apparent.

Some newborns' eyelids are slightly swollen because of pressure on the eyes during delivery. The swelling usually goes down in the first week. Others have small red spots in the white part of the eye, which also disappear in two to three weeks as the blood is reabsorbed into the body.

Blocked tear ducts, which can last from a few days to a few months, are common in newborns, too. If your baby seems to tear up frequently, wash your hands thoroughly, and, using your pointer finger, gently massage the inside corner of her eye. In more than 90 percent of the cases, the duct will open by itself within the first year, sometimes as a result of crying. If the duct doesn't open, your pediatrician might have to intervene.

Nose

At birth, your baby's nose might be a bit flattened, crooked, or dislocated, but these conditions usually remedy themselves. In a week or two, he won't look like an old prizefighter.

Breasts

Regardless of gender, babies can be born with swollen breasts, because they absorb their moms' hormones through the placenta. You'd see this in your baby during the first ten days. One of his breasts could be bigger than the other. Gradually, as he takes in breast milk or formula, the liquid flushes out the hormones, and the swelling goes down. One breast might remain swollen longer. Never press or squeeze your baby's breasts; they can become infected. If one or both breasts are red or sensitive to the touch, contact your pediatrician.

Skin

At birth, your baby came out with a white, waxy coating that protected her in your uterus. Her skin will be thin and possibly wrinkled. It's also normal for infants to have dry skin and to have some peeling on their hands and feet. I use a moisturizing product—a petroleum jelly, such as Vaseline or Aquaphor, or an unscented oil, sometimes olive oil. However, some pediatricians advise mothers to do nothing.

WHAT IF . . . My Baby's Skin Looks Yellow?

Babies who look yellow at birth or in the first few days usually have jaundice, a condition caused by an excess of bilirubin, the yellow pigment produced in the liver. It is not serious and is easily treated. Jaundice in babies is related to early feeding difficulties. Mom's milk comes in too slowly. Baby has trouble latching on or sucking. Mom has painful nipples. Any one of those possibilities means that the baby is ingesting only a small amount of liquid, not enough to flush out the bilirubin. His skin and the whites of his eyes turn yellow, which can be scary to a new mom.

The treatment is a combination of exposure to light and feedings around the clock—breast milk or formula—which will cause the yellow tone to fade. Put your baby near a sunny window for at least ten minutes every day. Be sure to protect her sensitive skin by positioning her out of direct sunlight.

During the day, feed her whenever she's hungry, ideally every two hours. (In this book, when I refer to the time between feedings, the clock starts when the prior feeding began. For example, if your baby started eating at seven A.M., and the next time she eats it's 9 A.M., that's two hours between feedings.) Babies with jaundice tend to sleep a lot, but don't let your baby skip a feeding. If necessary, wake her up. At night, continue to feed her at least every three hours. The more she ingests, the more she'll poop, which is how bilirubin is eliminated. You'll know she's getting enough liquid, because her diapers will be wet and her urine will be light.

Your pediatrician or nurse-practitioner should monitor your baby's progress during the first few days. If the above strategies don't relieve the condition, phototherapy—a light treatment—will probably be prescribed. Given in the hospital or at home, phototherapy speeds up the elimination of bilirubin. However, during treatment, which can last from a few hours to a week, your baby can lose as much as 25 percent of her body fluids. The possibility of dehydration is another reason to be especially vigilant about increasing the number of feedings.

Your Baby's Movements

Just as his body parts and brain will change after birth, it will take time for your baby's nervous system to mature. He will be utterly uncoordinated at first, making a variety of jerky, uncontrollable motions. You might, for example, notice tremors when you put him on the changing table. This is not only normal, but it also indicates that your baby's nervous system is working well. However, remember that what you see are primitive reflexes, automatic movements. Neanderthal babies did the same thing! Your baby isn't making these movements on purpose; he isn't trying to "say" something. However, each reflex is nature's way of helping your baby survive and get what he needs.

Sucking Reflex

Babies are programmed to eat. When anything touches your baby's lips, such as a nipple or when you insert a finger into his mouth, he will automatically start sucking. In low-birth-weight babies, the sucking reflex may not be very strong. Sucking also calms your baby.

Rooting Reflex

Rooting helps an infant find his mother's breast. If you run your finger along your baby's cheek or along the side of his mouth, he will turn his head and open his mouth in that direction, seeking something to suck. Rooting usually disappears in three or four months, but in some babies it lasts as long as a year.

Hand-to-Mouth Reflex

When you put light pressure on your baby's palm she will bend her arm, bring her hand to her mouth, and automatically start sucking. This reflex fades around three months. By then, your baby will have gained enough control over her arms to intentionally suck on her fingers and/or hand.

Tongue-Thrust Reflex

Touching a baby's lips causes his tongue to jut forward. I often use it to jump-start a "lazy" newborn. Once I've coaxed him to

WHAT REFLEXES SAY "HUNGRY"?

The sucking, rooting, hand-to-mouth, and tongue-thrust reflexes are all associated with eating but are not necessarily signs that your newborn is hungry. All babies need to suck, some more than others. So, while you should pay attention, don't rely solely on these automatic movements to determine whether your baby is hungry. Also look at the clock, especially during the first ten days. Your baby can nurse as often as every two hours if she wakes up on her own. If she is asleep, though, and three hours have passed since her last feeding, wake her up to give her a breast or a bottle.

open wider by rubbing the nipple along his upper and lower lips, I gently push the nipple into his mouth, which then activates his sucking reflex. Whereas tongue-thrust helps with liquid feeding, it works against taking in solid foods. Fortunately, it generally fades by three or four months. (If it remains active longer, as it does in some babies, it can make it difficult to introduce solids.)

Grasp Reflex

If you place your index finger in your newborn's palm, he will grab it and clench it in his fist. The grasp reflex disappears around three months. In the meantime, remember that when he grabs your finger, it's not because he doesn't want you to go or is afraid of being alone!

Moro Reflex

Your baby will look startled when you change his position abruptly, when you move suddenly, or when a sharp, loud sound rings out, such as a doorbell or a dog's bark. He isn't actually frightened, but his movements make him look as if he is. He cries and, at the same time, jerks with his whole body. His legs fly; he has no coordination. At times, he almost looks as if he's falling and is trying to grasp onto something. The Moro reflex can also occur when he's sleeping. It will disappear gradually after four to eight weeks.

Chapter 3

BONDING WITH YOUR BABY

I never get tired of watching a mother stare at her new baby. She looks at the little hands, the tiny feet. She runs loving fingers over the whole body, feeling the heartbeat in her palms. She listens to the breathing and the soft noises her baby makes. She inhales the "baby smell"—a distinct fragrance if there ever was one—as if it is a delicate flower.

In her baby's face, the mother can see traces of her husband or maybe a little of her parents or herself. The tiny creature who has been growing, moving, and kicking inside her for the last nine months is finally here. Mommy can now gaze into his eyes. This miracle is *her child*. The picture may be a bit different for an adoptive mother who has not carried the child inside her. But when that infant—now *her* baby—is placed in her arms for the first time, it activates a primitive maternal instinct: she wants to care for and protect her child.

A baby's arrival changes a woman's life forever and alters her days and nights in ways that she could never have imagined. Something inside her changes, too. I have seen many a mother "fall in love" with her baby, even though he was a "surprise" or didn't come at a "good time" or didn't fit neatly into her life plan. I have seen executive mothers, fully absorbed in careers, completely change their priorities after childbirth.

In fact, I would have to say that with few exceptions, almost every new mother I've ever met exhibits deep affection for her baby. Often, but not always, this is true from the first moment they see each other.

Perhaps you've already experienced this yourself. But if your baby hasn't yet arrived, let me tell you that the connection between you and your newborn can feel so encompassing that it will seem as if nothing exists except you and the tender, small being in your arms—nothing but love.

The Maternal Bond

Your baby will quickly come to know your smell and recognize your voice. Her little hands will reach for your face. Although no one is quite sure *how* your baby senses the love you have for her, she does. She is a long way from talking, but she knows and depends on you to feed her and care for her.

At first, you are all your baby needs. Because of your nurturing, she will become secure enough to venture out on her own. Some scientists say that "attachment"—this dance of love— explains how humans evolved.

Thousands and thousands of years ago, babies would not have survived without their mothers. While the men went out hunting, the women had babies, fed them from their breasts, and stayed close to the young to protect them from harsh weather, wild animals, and other dangers. All babies in the animal kingdom, including those early humans, are endowed with an innate power to "pull" their mothers in. They cry when they are hungry or cold or in pain, and they rely on primitive reflexes to get what they need. The babies most likely to survive and to pass on their genes are those who stay close to their mothers.

Modern babies are no different. Reeling you in is part of your baby's genetic makeup, handed down from your ancestors. Today, mothers don't have to be scared of wild animals stealing their babies. And technology has given us formula, so that feeding can be done by anyone. But if taking care of a newborn were merely a combination of accomplishing routine tasks that might someday be handled by a robot, my life's work would have no meaning. Babies need love to live and thrive. Therefore, this first phase of motherhood is about forming a bond of trust with your baby.

When you hear your baby cry, you go to her, talk softly, and hold her close to your body. She is calmed by your touch and feels connected to you. She's your baby cub, and you are the mama lion. It is as if the two of you are encased in a cocoon—you become one.

Mommy and Me

Watch any baby who is just beginning to crawl. The one who is "securely attached"—he trusts that his mother is there to care for him—will venture across the room to get a toy. But he keeps looking back. If Mom smiles, he keeps going. No words are passed between them, but their connection is obvious. Scientists call this the "affective bond."

Similarly, a toddler who feels insecure in an unfamiliar place—say, a new play group or day-care facility—will initially grab his mother's leg. It's almost as if holding on to her is a way of recharging his battery. After a few minutes, when he's sure she's not going to leave him, his curiosity takes over. He lets go. But he keeps looking back at her, even as he explores.

But what happens when Mom is not there? Let's say you have

to go to another room. You would first make sure that your baby is safe on his own; put him into his crib or strap him into his infant seat. And before you walk out, you'd tell him, "I'll be right back."

OK, Mom, I get that you're laughing at me. I can imagine you thinking, *We're talking about a one-week-old baby, Luiza!* But I say this. Get into the habit of allowing him to be alone and of explaining things to him. Let him know you're there for him. It's important to be honest with your child from the day you bring him home. This is how he learns to trust you.

So, no, it's not too early. Hugging him and talking to him helps him learn that you sometimes disappear but also come back. Even these first few days matter in terms of attachment and trust. Here's why.

You are a mirror for your baby. Babies are born with feelings they can't identify: pleasure and discomfort. In the reflection of your eyes, your baby will begin to understand what he sees around him. We don't know exactly when babies start to understand language, but we do know that they can sense emotions from the moment they are born. Your smile tells him that the world is safe. When you quietly say, "There, there, you'll be fine," or "You're just hungry," you comfort him. Reassuring him like this will help him make sense of his new, strange environment.

You get to know how your baby acts and reacts. No two infants are alike. Some babies come into the world more fearful, more sensitive, or more feisty than others. It is important to know it's not your "fault" if your baby is a "crier" or a "bad sleeper" or "tense." To be sure, you and your partner—and previous generations in both your families—have passed down genes that affect his temperament. Even so, you can neither take credit for your baby's so-called good qualities nor take blame for his less desirable characteristics. Still, mothering requires a great deal of effort and responsibility. After all, it is you who will provide the kind of environment that brings out the best of who your child is. You must remind yourself to be attentive, patient, and open. In time, you will get to know what he's like and what he likes.

You give your baby her first voice. Babies communicate with their whole bodies. When a mother is attuned to her baby, she is able to interpret wordless communication. It doesn't happen overnight. I, having cared for hundreds of babies, need at least two weeks to understand what a new baby wants. But by having your child on a good routine, which we'll discuss soon, and by paying attention, you learn a lot. Look and listen; watch her body language. She, in turn, learns by watching you. You will also understand each other, even when no words are used. And before you know it, she will understand real words and, in time, begin to use them.

You both become more confident. This is perhaps the most wonderful by-product of the maternal bond. When you are able to correctly interpret your baby's needs, you gain confidence, and you are better able to handle whatever challenge comes your way. When your baby's needs are met, he gains confidence, too. It's a reinforcing loop: the better a mother you are, the better a mother you become.

But I'm Not "Maternal"

There is no way to teach a person how to love another person. But I know I can teach you how to tune in. Even if you don't think you're ready for the job, I promise you that nature will step in, and something special will happen once you allow yourself to be open to the experience of motherhood.

Admittedly, a very small percentage of women don't want the challenge. Such a woman might have received no love and attention as a child, and by the time she's an adult, she feels too vulnerable to open herself to an infant. Or perhaps she feels that her life is full as it is. Her other roles—manager, partner, artist, musician—leave no time for motherhood. Whatever the reason a woman doesn't want children, that is certainly her right.

Another reason it's hard for some women to step into the new role of mother is that society doesn't always value the job. When one is asked, "What do you do?" the answer "I'm a mother" doesn't get the same respect as "I'm a lawyer" or "I'm a pianist." *Just a mother?*

Even among women who do want to have children, not all are instantly comfortable in the role. To be sure, it's love at first sight for some new mothers. From the first moment, holding their baby feels natural and easy. But many women are far less confident in the beginning. They need time to get used to the role and to "fall in love" with their babies. I saw this in my early days as a baby nurse in Brazil. That's why I never kept new mothers away from their babies, as German nurses typically did. I wanted to teach, not take over. After all, at some point I would leave, and Mom would have to care for her own baby.

Even today, when I join a family, I always remind the mother that, yes, I can help her learn how to diaper and feed her baby. I can wake up to give him that four A.M. bottle. But I can't be a replacement for her maternal love. And long after I leave the household, her connection to that baby will continue to be crucial to his emotional development.

The early days of motherhood are particularly difficult for women who haven't been around infants or had any experience with their care—no younger siblings, no baby-sitting jobs. We don't teach mothering in school. A woman might have an important job or special talents that have made her successful and even well known, but many of those skills don't transfer to motherhood. She can be utterly lost when it comes to her baby's care.

Perhaps you immediately rose to the challenge. If, on the other hand, you've convinced yourself that you're "not maternal," be patient. You're understandably frightened by the responsibility of caring for such a vulnerable creature. You might also be upset by the crying and the persistent sense of not knowing what to do or what comes next. But I encourage you, as I have so many women, to remember my essential principles. Be patient. Try to take the time to pay attention. Open yourself to the experience.

I assure you—and I have seen this time and again—that your baby has the primitive power to pull you in. Even though you feel anxious or reluctant now, when you give her day-by-day love and care, a relationship will gradually develop and deepen.

Let's not sugarcoat this, however. A baby is a symbol of joy and happiness, but he is also a promise of constant demands, interrupted sleep, or no sleep at all. When your baby cries and you can't soothe him, it can unsettle the whole family, sometimes even the neighbors. But know that you're not alone. Every woman, even the "earth mother" type you met on the maternity ward, has moments of doubt and confusion. After all, no one has ever taught you how to act in or handle this situation.

A wise mother once told me that to have a baby is to be condemned to live one day at a time. It's reward enough to get through the day with nothing bad happening! This is particularly true in the first three months of your baby's life, when every day is new and filled with new challenges.

WHAT IF . . . I'm Not Happy About Being a Mother?

You feel exhausted, frightened, discouraged, confused—or all of the above? You're grinning one minute and fuming the next? Somewhere between 50 percent and 80 percent of all mothers experience variations of the "baby blues" within a few days after their babies are born. It is *not* the same as postpartum depression (PPD). Baby blues start almost immediately and usually disappear by the third week. PPD, on the other hand, is a form of clinical depression that takes longer to emerge and can go on for months. It's not a case of temporary mood swings.

You're *not* doing this to yourself. Having the baby blues, in part, is a biological response to rapid changes in your hormone levels. But it's also a response to your exhaustion and the physical toll on your body, not to mention the realization that you are now responsible for another human being. You might even struggle with feelings of guilt. You think you *should* be more comfortable in this new role. You *should* be in love with your baby. You *should* be doing more. You *should* get back to work.

The problem is, you don't feel like yourself. You lack energy; even after a nap, you feel tired. You might have strange food cravings or have no appetite. You're nervous, confused, discouraged, overwhelmed. You cry easily and frequently. At times, you find it difficult to think clearly. Worst of all, you might even wonder if you really love your baby.

Although these feelings are scary when you're going through them, they go with the territory. During the next six weeks or so, your hormones will begin to adjust to your postbaby body. In the meantime, find a shoulder to cry on—a loved one or a friend (ideally, another mother). New-mother groups help, too. Just as important, try to see this as a hurdle, not a life sentence. Six or eight weeks from now, you will be more accustomed to your new role. Everything *will* be forever different, but I promise that the routine will feel familiar, and you'll begin to regain a sense of control. If not, and you continue to feel anxious, you might be experiencing early signs of PPD, which would warrant a call to your doctor. Particularly if you have a history of clinical depression, this might be more serious than a rough patch.

Chapter 4

BEING WITH YOUR NEWBORN

You will eventually be able to get your baby on a routine. But for now, your newborn will mostly eat and sleep. You were together for the last nine months. You know her better than you think. Take it one day at a time, and just *be* with her. Get people to help, and don't expect that anything is going to be the way it once was.

Follow the Baby—and Pay Attention

In these first precious days at home, let your baby take the lead, and keep her close. She gets to know your scent and the feel of your body. You learn to "read" her and enjoy the miracle she is.

When your baby is hungry, she should eat. Don't put her on the clock. We can't "schedule" newborns; it goes against biology. A healthy baby will let you know when she is hungry. Feed her whenever she starts "rooting" for food, searching for anything that she can suck on. In a few weeks, we will start guiding your baby toward a routine, but at this point, just listen to what she's "telling" you. Make a mental note, or, better, write down the times she feeds and sleeps. She might want to eat every two hours, manage to stretch it out to three, or sometimes last only an hour between feedings. (Remember, we're counting from the *beginning* of the previous feeding.) She'll let you know what she needs. Pay attention.

You will feed her, change her diaper, and continue feeding her around the clock. In between, you will hold her and look into her eyes. Most newborns stay awake for only a half hour at a time when they first come home from the hospital. Whenever she's tired, she should sleep.

In these early days, as you (and your partner) get to know your baby, observe how she reacts to her new environment. Notice whether she's sensitive to lights or loud noises. Does she twitch frequently? Does she seem as if she's in pain after eating? Does she seem to cry a lot? To answer such questions, keep her constantly in your sight.

One reason I stress *being* with your baby is that some newborns need a little more help to feel comfortable. Another reason is so you can keep an eye out for danger signs. For example, some newborns tend to vomit in the first few days. If you had a normal childbirth and your baby had no problems, you were probably released from the hospital a day later. However, some infants are not thoroughly aspirated, a process done in the delivery room to clear the trachea of mucus. Once at home, a baby who was improperly aspirated might throw up thick mucus, which also can interfere with his breathing when he's lying down. This particular type of vomiting diminishes after the first few days. If the baby eats at least every three hours, the liquid dilutes the mucus.

Your baby's temperament also plays an important role, not just now but always. Some newborns are "good as gold"—relaxed, even-tempered, and easy to care for. They sleep and eat well, cry only when they are hungry or uncomfortable, and go back to sleep as soon as their needs are met. At the other extreme are what I call "difficult-to-calm" newborns, babies who tend to have a rough homecoming. They complain by crying—sometimes a lot of crying. They might have digestion problems or sensitivities right from the beginning. Some have trouble finding a good position to sleep. Others give the impression that they are sleeping, but it's probably more accurate to say they pass out, exhausted from the stress of uninterrupted crying. (You'll read more about these babies in chapter 15.)

Most newborns fall somewhere between the two extremes. If your baby is calm most of the time, feeds well, and sleeps well, great! But if he is extremely active and sensitive, agitated in new situations, and/or fussy most of the time, the best thing you can do is to show him what comfort feels like. He's been sloshing cozily inside you. He still needs your company and love.

Lie with him in your bed or on a comfortable chair with a foot rest that allows you to recline partially. Lay him facedown on your chest so he can hear the beating of your heart, a sound already familiar to him. This will keep his body temperature steady and synchronize his breathing with yours, which will calm him and help him sleep.

I don't believe in holding babies all the time, nor am I a fan of the family bed. But if there's ever a phase of motherhood when I think it's good just to *be* with your baby and not worry about overdoing it, it's now. Don't be afraid of being with her "too much" or worry whether you're becoming a "helicopter mom." Instead, see these next ten days as an opportunity to bond and teach your baby how to trust.

Whether you continue to allow your baby to sleep in your bed is another matter. It depends on your lifestyle, how your partner feels about it, your baby's needs, the size of your house and family, and your philosophy about child-rearing. Some mothers who practice "attachment parenting" believe that sleeping with their babies is the best way to bond and to promote healthy emotional development. However, as I stressed earlier, attachment comes from love and connection, not co-sleeping.

Whichever route you take, make a *conscious* decision about it. Babies quickly get used to patterns of care. The older yours gets, the harder it will be for her to adapt to sleeping alone. So if you don't want to continue co-sleeping, start getting her accustomed to her bassinet or crib by slowly phasing in short periods of separation during the day. As you become more settled and familiar with your baby's wants and needs, you can be less vigilant but still keep tabs on her by using a baby monitor.

What to Do About the Crying

When you hear the word "newborn," what immediately comes to mind? Crying! All babies cry. Even calm infants fuss and cry from time to time. A new mother has to get used to crying.

It's your baby's way of "talking" to you, telling you what he needs. The problem is that this week, all your baby's wails will sound the same to you.

Let's say your baby pulls up his legs and lets out a wail. What does it mean? What does he need? His face gets red, and you can't calm him. You try. You feed him . . . again. Then he cries even harder. Now what? You might wonder, *Is something wrong with my milk? Am I a bad mother? Oh, God, maybe I ate something that is causing him so much pain.*

Instead of panicking, do as I do. Take your time. Although your heart races whenever your baby cries, try to stay calm. As I always tell my clients, "If we are nervous, the baby will be nervous, too."

It's not always hunger. The first thing we assume when we hear a baby cry is that she's hungry, so we feed her. But that's not always what she needs. Babies sometimes cry because they feel uncomfortable or are in pain. They cry when they're too hot or too cold. They cry when they're tired or overstimulated. If you're breast-feeding, your baby might cry because she is having trouble latching on or sucking.

Talk to your baby. I talk to babies just the way I talk to you. In the middle of the night, I try to be as quiet and invisible as possible. But during of the day, I reassure in a soft voice, reciting a string of calming phrases, such as, *Meu amor, porque esta chora-deira? A vida e boa . . . você e uma criança feliz* ("My love, why are you crying? Life is good . . . you are a happy child!"). I speak Portuguese not only because it's natural for me but also because exposing a baby to a variety of sounds is good for his developing brain. It doesn't matter what you say, as long as you talk to your baby from day one. He will soon associate your voice with safety and well-being, and that will calm him when he's crying.

Observe your home from your baby's perspective. We don't get to choose whether we have an easy baby or a difficult-to-calm one or any of the variations in between. But we can be respectful of the baby's temperament and figure out what kind of environment will make him cry *less.* For instance, if your baby is fussy and gets irritated with lots of stimulation, provide a calmer environment. Don't come at him too fast; he will do better when he's not as-saulted by too many toys, bright lights, loud music, and a parade of visitors.

Make sure your baby gets enough sleep. Parents tend to keep newborns awake for longer than they should. The baby seems happy, she's not crying, and everyone wants to hold her and rock her and make goo-goo noises in her face. Also, some people be-lieve that the less a baby sleeps during the day, the better she will sleep at night. I hear that often, but it's *dead wrong.* Babies need rest, lots of it. When your baby gets overtired, her immature ner-vous system cannot cope with stimulation, so she cries. Take her to a quiet place, swaddle her (see below), and keep her on your chest until she falls asleep. Giving her something to suck on will also help calm her. If you're bottle-feeding, introduce a pacifier; if you're nursing, let her suck on your pinkie finger.

Remember that crying goes with the territory. It's tricky to talk about crying by itself, because it's always linked to something your baby needs. But I can tell you that what *you* do matters. Stay calm, and don't take his crying personally—he's not "angry" at you, he doesn't "think" you're a bad mother. Talk to him; reassure him. Most important, put his crying in perspective. It won't last forever.

Swaddling = Sleep

The minute your baby is born, she will have a fairly regular sleep cycle of two to three hours at a stretch. Of course, this is day *and* night, which means that it will be a while before *you* have a good night's sleep, or at least some solid sleep. During the first few days, most babies are angels. They sleep and nurse.

But even when newborns are angels during the first ten days, it is not wise to let them sleep for more than four hours during the night, because they need the nutrition that comes from being fed. In the first three or four days outside the womb, newborns normally lose 5 percent of their birth weight if they're fed formula and as much as 7 percent if they're breast-fed.

No matter what you hear, "sleeping through the night" during the first ten days is a myth. *All* newborns require around-the-clock feeding, *at least* eight times in a twenty-four-hour period at first. When I hear that a week-old baby is "such an angel" or "a good sleeper," I worry. I haven't met a healthy baby who lasts even six hours in the first ten days (or in the first month, for that matter). That "good" baby might be dehydrated, fighting jaundice, or weak because he isn't getting proper nutrition. At worst, he might end up in the emergency room.

Infants need their sleep, between seventeen and twenty hours a day at first. At two weeks, most healthy babies start to stay awake longer between feedings. The most important consideration now, though, is to get your baby back to her birth weight, so you'll interrupt her sleep, even in the middle of the night. But take heart. The way your baby sleeps this week is *not* how she'll sleep in the weeks to come. In the meantime, you can take steps to make your baby's sleep more peaceful, the most important being swaddling.

All newborns twitch when they sleep, which can cause their arms to flail about. But as I explained earlier, they have no control over their movements. Observe your baby when she's lying down. When she waves her arms, she has no idea that they're even hers! When she's asleep, the feeling of her own hand on her face can wake her. And the sight of her arms zipping in and out of her field of vision can prevent her from going back to sleep.

What to do? Swaddle her entire body in a cotton blanket that prevents her arms from flailing. Buying a blanket specifically made for swaddling is a good investment. You will use it during the first and second months, or until those jerky movements start to subside. Swaddling is essential to newborn comfort. It helps your little one sleep longer, because she's wrapped up, as cozy as she was inside your body. Particularly if you have a very active baby, she will wake up more frequently if you don't swaddle her.

Although I cover sleep rituals more fully in chapter 12, start now to:

> ‣ Maintain a calm environment before putting your baby down. Change the tone of your voice, and get her out of the hustle and bustle of the household.

> ‣ Darken her room.

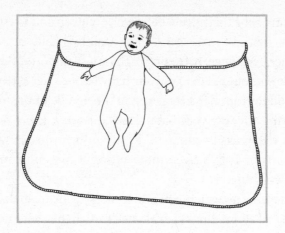

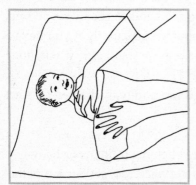

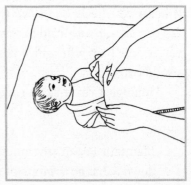

› Swaddle her, arms tucked in.

› Place her on her back, with her face turned opposite the side she was sleeping on before. To keep track, always lay her down on the same side as you used for breast-feeding. If you gave her your right breast, her face will be turned toward her right side.

If your newborn is restless and uncomfortable in the beginning, she will require much more of your affection and attention. Hold her until she calms down, but try to place her in her bed *before* she falls asleep. If necessary, repeat this until she finally sleeps.

Your Sleep and Care

The calm of this first ten days is not just for the baby. You have needs, too. Your body is in recovery stage. Remember how my mother cared for the new mothers in our neighborhood? She put them in *quarentena*—rest and relaxation, with no responsibilities—for forty days after their babies' birth. Do the same for yourself. Eat foods that restore you and comfort you, such as chicken soup, and include lots of protein in your diet for energy.

Your only worry should be to care for your little one and give your own body a chance to heal. No lifting, no stress. This will also help get your milk flowing if you breast-feed, which I hope you'll at least try.

Most important, sleep when your baby sleeps. Don't worry about writing thank-you notes or checking your email. Keep company to a minimum, until you all settle in. If you don't learn how to take care of yourself, it's going to be a lot harder to take care of your baby.

WHAT IF . . . I Had a C-Section?

You might have a more difficult homecoming than a woman who's had an uncomplicated vaginal delivery. After any kind of surgery, gas, which can be extremely painful, tends to get trapped in your abdominal cavity. The site of your incision might be sore and tender, too. To make matters worse, you're recovering at a time when you're exhausted, confused, and, most likely, trying to learn how to breast-feed.

Walking around the house can help alleviate the pressure or at least move the gas around. Your discomfort *will* subside. In the meantime, try to relax and stay calm. Get someone to help with the baby or with house chores, if possible. If no one is available, this is the one circumstance where I think it's OK to bring your baby into your bed so that you don't have the additional stress of lifting her for feedings. However, it's safer to lay her down next to you, *not* between you and your partner.

Spread the Joy

Although you should keep visitors to a minimum this week, you should turn to your closest loved ones—the select few who offer the right kind of help. If you're honest with them and allow yourself not to be in charge (for once!), it will ease your mind and unburden you. Life is not the way it used to be. This week, you need help. Enlist your partner, Grandma, and whoever else is willing to pitch in. Let them hold and cuddle the baby. They'll love it, and although you are undoubtedly your baby's favorite face—her lifeline—she will love other faces, too. In fact, during the first few days, your newborn will benefit from spending time lying on anyone—male or female—who is willing to show her warmth and affection.

Men, of course, can be loving nurturers. My clients Brian and Doug hired a surrogate to carry their first baby. But when Kian arrived, they were right there in the delivery room. They both cut the umbilical cord. They took turns cradling their new son, bare chest to bare chest. The surrogate pumped her breast milk for a few weeks so that little Kian would get the health benefits. Brian is the stay-at-home parent, and he and Doug seemed to work out a nice balance between them.

If you're the mom (or, in the case of lesbians, the birth parent), and your partner offers to help without you having to ask, good for you, and good for your relationship! If not, let Dad (or your partner) know that you need help. Have him/her read the "Dear Dad/Partner" box below. It will open up a great discussion. Believe me, your significant other's help and understanding will make life easier for both of you.

Many new moms also rely on their mothers, and that's a great thing. Other than Dad, who is usually the most excited about the new baby? (No insult to grandfathers intended!) Whether mother and daughter see eye-to-eye depends, first of all, on how they got along in the past. If you're close to your mother and agree on most things, great. If not, having a baby gives you a chance to repair your relationship.

Either way, try to listen to each other. Your mother probably did things differently in her day, and some of her suggestions might not be helpful. She might or might not have breast-fed. She might question why you always put your baby to sleep on his back. She certainly didn't have all the equipment and safety precautions we have now. In any case, don't overreact to her different opinion. It's just her opinion. Do tell her what you need. She can hold the baby for you. She can keep an eye on things when you nap. She can shop and cook for you.

Depending on the size of your family and your friend network and whether people who are emotionally close to you also live nearby, you might have a few or lots of others to call on. Now's the time to connect with them. Every new mom needs help. Good for you if you made a friend on the maternity ward. She might not be able to provide physical help—she's got her own baby to deal with—but your babies are exactly the same age, so it might be good at least to talk to her and see how and what she is doing.

DEAR DAD/PARTNER . . .

Hold the baby after feedings or when he is crying. It's not just to give Mommy a break; it's to get acquainted with the newest member of your family.

Offer to do at least one of the nighttime feedings. If your baby is breast-fed, you can take part once she drinks from a bottle.

Sing your baby to sleep. Songs calm infants, and, believe it or not, singing calms fathers, too.

Bring the new mommy breakfast in bed. She is exhausted after waking up so many times during the night.

Learn how to change diapers. If Mommy looks over your shoulder to see whether you're doing it right, calmly say, "Thanks, hon, but I've got this."

Take over most of the domestic chores, or hire someone to do them. Mommy needs as much rest as she can get, for at least the next two weeks; longer if she's had a C-section.

Be patient. Understand that new mothers are often fragile, among other reasons, because their hormones are unbalanced.

Don't worry if you feel a little awkward at first with "mothering" tasks. Be honest about your own anxieties, and just try to do your best.

Use common sense. You will have to make adjustments to your everyday routine. Nothing stays the same when a baby joins a household.

Be kind to yourself, too. You'll learn through practice and experience. If you are loving, flexible, gentle, and strong—and keep the spotlight off yourself—you are already on your way to becoming an excellent co-parent (and partner).

Chapter 5

A CLEAN START

When you first come home from the hospital, you have to jump right in. Daily "maintenance" is up to you now, and you might have to start mastering new skills—such as diapering. You also have to learn how to clean your baby's tender little parts without actually giving her a bath. If you know what to expect and what to look for, it makes the job of caring for and cleaning your little bundle of joy a lot easier.

Diapering

Diapering is one of the most basic, essential skills to learn. The average newborn requires at least ten to twelve diaper changes a day, more if your baby happens to pee or poop *during* a diaper change. The important part of diapering is to make sure that (1) you clean the baby properly, (2) the diaper is positioned correctly on the baby's waist, and (3) you don't make a mess while doing it. Here's how I do it:

› Don't take the diaper off right away. Instead, fold it under your baby so that the dirty part is now covered. This creates a sort of shelf that elevates the baby's tush a little and makes it easier to wipe, because the baby's bottom is tilted up a bit.

› Wipe from top (below the belly button) to bottom (toward the anus). Never go back and forth.

› If the area is not completely clean, repeat the process, but use a new wipe.

› When your baby's cute little bottom is clean, instead of putting a new diaper on right away, either fan the area with your hand or dry it with white tissue (never colored).

› To protect against diaper rash, apply a coat of petroleum jelly, such as Aquaphor or Vaseline, around the area, or a diaper cream. If necessary, try a few brands to find what works best.

› Flap your hands like a butterfly, palms down, to smooth open a new diaper, and keep it down. Gently slip the clean diaper under the baby, aligning the top with the baby's waist.

› When you close the diaper on your baby's belly, make sure it isn't too tight. Slip your hand halfway down the front of the diaper (palm out, so that the back of your hand is on your baby's belly).

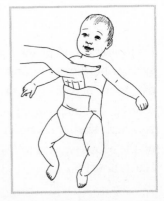

Don't worry if you don't get it right at first. But at least try to do it the same way each time, and I promise it will soon seem easy.

Diaper Warning Signs

What's in and under your baby's diaper can tell you a lot about what's going on in her body.

Dark stools. As your baby starts to take in food and her digestive system gets going, she will poop frequently and quickly. What comes out initially will be watery and have a brownish-green or dark green color. This is normal. In part, it's because she's secreting meconium, a thick, dark, sticky substance stored in her body before birth. The more breast milk or formula she consumes, the faster she will pass the meconium.

Diaper rash. Your baby's skin is new and delicate. Wiping her bottom to clean the meconium can make her skin raw. Having a bright red bottom is very painful for your baby; every time you change her, it's like rubbing a fresh burn. Severe diaper rash can happen very fast. When it does, instead of wiping the area, clean your baby's bottom in the sink. When my babies have diaper rashes, I put a teaspoon of cornstarch into a small container with around eight ounces of water. It's a trick my mother taught me, and it helps the skin heal more quickly. Pat dry, and before putting on a new diaper, instead of using Aquaphor, Vaseline, or your usual everyday ointment, try something thicker that acts as a barrier to the moisture, such as a triple antibiotic ointment. Also ask your pediatrician for a recommendation.

Dark urine. When your newborn starts nursing, the colostrum that comes before breast milk begins to show up in her diaper. At first, it's just a drop, and then it increases. Eventually, you start to get very wet diapers. However, if your baby has difficulty latching on or if your milk is delayed for more than three days, he won't have much liquid in his diaper, and it will be dark. You might also see little crystals instead of liquid. The diaper is "telling" you that your baby is not getting enough nutrition and might also become dehydrated. This isn't a reason to panic. Just keep an eye on his diapers. If they're dry for more than a day or two, especially if you're not supplementing with formula, call your pediatrician.

Giving a Sponge Bath

Until your baby's umbilical cord falls off, his body can't be submerged in water. So we need to clean him, without actually giving him a bath. Instead, we do a "sponge bath," while he's lying on the changing table or any padded surface that's comfortable for you. You'll need a bowl of warm water, a small soft washcloth, and a soft bath towel. Use baby soap or an unscented soap for the diaper area.

Warm up the room before you undress your baby. You don't have to wash his head every time, but when you do, wash it first. Wrap him in a towel and hold him with his feet under your arm, supporting his head in your hand.

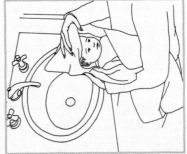

Wash his hair gently with baby shampoo. Brushing the scalp with a soft-bristled brush will help get rid of the dry skin. Dry his head well with the towel, and then continue to sponge off the rest of his body.

Start with his upper body. On days you're not washing his head, just take his shirt off. Place a dry towel over the parts you're not washing. Use the moist cloth, first to clean his face, then his arms, underarms, back, and chest.

Dry his skin gently. Be especially careful to dry areas where his skin folds, such as inside his elbow and under his neck. Put on a clean onesie or shirt. Repeat this with his bottom, cleaning his genitals, legs, and around the umbilical cord.

Usually a sponge bath will relax your baby, so do it after a feeding and before his next period of sleep. It is too early to start baby massage, but when he's wrapped up in the towel you can press down gently on his arms and legs. Your baby will feel secure having your hands on his body.

Care of the Umbilical Cord

Minutes after your baby was born, your obstetrician or your partner cut the umbilical cord that connected you and your baby while she was in your uterus. It left a little "stump" on her belly that is approximately three-quarters of an inch long. It takes about two to three weeks, sometimes up to a month, for the umbilical stump to dry up and fall off. In its place, a layer of fine skin will be created, her future "belly button." Check with your pediatrician, but most advise against immersing babies in water until the stump falls off. Here's what else you need to remember:

> › Keep the area around the stump uncovered and dry to let it heal naturally.

> Most newborn disposable diapers have a little cut-out feature in front that leaves the belly button exposed. But if your diapers do not, take care at each diaper change to fold down the front of the diaper, from inside out, so it doesn't rub against the stump.

> It is normal to have a little blood when the stump is ready to fall off. Dab it with a cotton ball moistened with warm water.

Infection of the umbilical cord and navel area are rare, but it can happen when bacteria enters through the open orifice. And although it's unlikely, if your baby's umbilical area becomes red or oozes a puslike secretion with a bad odor, contact your pediatrician immediately.

Special Hygiene Issues for Boys and Girls

Boys

Circumcision is a surgical procedure in which the foreskin that surrounds the tip of the penis is removed. It is done on more than half of all boy babies, according to the U.S. Centers for Disease Control. It used to be done routinely, but circumcision has actually declined in the last few years. Some parents and doctors question whether it should be done at all. Although it is easier to maintain good hygiene of a circumcised penis, and some studies claim that removal of the foreskin can be instrumental in preventing certain diseases, not everyone considers circumcision a necessity. It's a very personal decision, one I can't help my clients make. My advice is to learn all you can about circumcision and then decide what's best for your baby.

If your baby boy was not circumcised, do not force the skin

of the penis backward to clean it. Water and mild soap are enough.

If your baby boy was circumcised, here are some things to keep in mind immediately after the procedure:

> It is often easier to calm your baby if he is tightly swaddled. Breast-feeding can also help calm him.

> Remove the bandage—usually a simple gauze dressing— within twenty-four to forty-eight hours, or as instructed by your doctor or *mohel*, a person trained to perform circumcisions. If the bandage falls off by itself, it's usually not necessary to replace it.

> Once the dressing has been removed, at each diaper change make a "ring" of petroleum jelly on a square of gauze and place it on top of your baby's penis. This will prevent the raw skin from being rubbed by, or sticking to, the diaper.

> Once a day, using a cotton swab dipped in petroleum jelly, push back the skin, similar to the way you'd push back a nail cuticle. This helps the new skin heal without gluing itself to the penis.

> If your baby's genitals are contaminated by poop, use warm water to clean the area. Let it dry well, and repeat the procedure of applying the petroleum jelly before putting on a clean diaper.

The healing process lasts about one week, but if your baby's umbilical cord is still intact, wait until it falls off before immersing him in water.

Girls

Always wipe from front to back, or toward the anus. You might have to apply a little more pressure to clean the area after a poop. Some baby girls also have a clear or white vaginal discharge, caused by their mothers' hormones. Don't be concerned. Just keep the vaginal area clean—again, by wiping from front to back. However, if the discharge is yellow or green, or if it seems excessive, call your pediatrician.

Chapter 6

—

FEEDING BASICS

Your baby is a little eating machine. That's her job. Your job is to make sure she gets enough to eat. In chapter 1, I helped you consider your choices—breast-feeding or formula-feeding. (In this book, I use the term "formula-feeding" instead of "bottle-feeding," because we can also feed breast milk from a bottle.) My recommendation is that you at least try breast-feeding, but I also recognize that not every woman can or wants to breast-feed. It upsets me to watch people *tsk-tsk* because a new mother gives her baby formula. You're not a "failure" if you choose to formula-feed or have to supplement your baby's diet. Most important, I want to put your mind at ease: when it comes to bonding and sharing special moments with your baby, *what* you feed her is less important than *how* you feed her.

With any feeding regimen, these first ten days are critical and, sometimes, challenging. I devote the next chapter to breast-feeding and discuss formula-feeding below. But first, let me answer your questions about feeding in general. Getting off to a good start will help you avoid the pitfalls.

First-Week Feeding Questions

No matter what or how or where you feed your baby, be patient, calm, and focused. Feeding is not a time to catch up on phone calls or check your email. Sit in a quiet place, away from the bustle of the household. Relish the contact and connection with your baby. Feedings go better when you are relaxed and comfortable. The experience will be emotionally satisfying for both of you.

The first ten days are a time of learning how the feeding regimen you have chosen works and understanding what your baby prefers. This is also critical in terms of your baby's weight.

THE WEIGH-IN

Your pediatrician will weigh your baby at three days and then again two weeks after delivery. On the second appointment, the doctor wants to make sure that your little one hasn't lost more than 10 percent of his birth weight and that he is at least beginning to put weight on, which indicates that he's getting adequate nutrition. Regaining the lost weight fully, though, could take another two to three weeks.

It also depends on the feeding method. Breast-fed babies typically lose more weight than formula-fed infants, because they initially take in less than formula-fed babies. It takes more time and effort for a baby to extract milk from a breast than from a silicone nipple, and it also takes time for Mom's milk to come in. In the meantime, you don't have to obsess about his weight. Just take the time to give him a good start. Trust me, the effort and attention you put in this week will pay off in the months to come.

With so much dependent on feeding, new mothers often have many questions. Here are the ones I get the most:

How often do I feed my baby? Whether they're fed breast milk or formula, most newborns eat between eight and twelve times during a twenty-four-hour period. But I don't schedule newborn feedings. So at this point, don't worry about how often you feed your baby, especially if you're breast-feeding. As I explained earlier, these first few days at home are a time to *follow* your baby. Respond quickly to her cries of hunger, and feed her "on demand." Remember, you're showing her that her needs will be met. She will let you know when she is hungry and stop sucking when she's full. Given their tiny stomachs, most newborns can only take in an ounce or two per feeding at first.

After the first ten days, many babies begin to space out their feedings in longer intervals—up to two hours apart for breast-fed infants, up to three hours apart for formula-fed (these differences later disappear). And with each feeding, you will get a little better at the basics and become more confident. The important thing is to establish good habits and take steps to avoid problems. *Vamos devagar ate acertar,* "Little by little . . . until you get it right."

How long should a feeding last? Most bottle-fed newborns finish their two ounces in fifteen to twenty minutes. Breast-feeding, at first, can take twenty to forty minutes. If your baby fusses right after a feeding, it could be that he's eating too fast. He takes in air along with liquid, and that can cause abdominal pain.

How do I know if my baby's getting enough to eat? Feeding formula involves less guesswork, because you can see how much he's consumed. I suggest starting with three-ounce bottles. During the first few days, your baby will take an ounce or two, which is all his tiny tummy (the size of his fist) can handle. He will gradually increase his capacity over the next two weeks, taking in eighteen to twenty ounces over a twenty-four-hour period. I don't like to overfeed. Use common sense, and trust yourself. When you breast-feed, it's trickier to gauge amounts. If your baby has been on your breast from twenty to forty minutes, that's usually sufficient for a feeding at the beginning. However, breast-milk production is not consistent. In the morning, your milk supply is higher than in the evening. It also depends on whether your baby is sucking properly and whether your body is manufacturing enough milk—issues I cover in the next chapter.

How often do I have to burp my baby? All babies, to varying degrees, ingest air while sucking. Burping—helping your baby expel that air—is an important part of the feeding. Some newborns have a tendency to spit up, and a good burp can help prevent them from regurgitating portions of the ingested milk. Burping can also ease gas pains and other tummy troubles.

Knowing exactly when to burp your baby is more art than science—it's all part of getting to know your baby. If your formula-fed baby doesn't give a signal that he needs to burp, a good rule of thumb is to take a break approximately fifteen minutes into the feeding. After he burps, allow him to continue eating until he's satisfied. Particularly with a breast-fed baby, it's not usually a good idea to break up a feeding. You'd spend all your waking hours breast-feeding, and it would exhaust you.

Some babies burp easily; others do not. In the middle of a feeding, if your baby squirms, stops sucking, or begins to cry—all signs that can mean he's uncomfortable—he probably needs to burp. Or if your baby finishes feeding, and when you lay him down he starts to move around or even cry, he probably needs to burp. Experiment with these three burping positions:

> *Seated.* Put him on your lap, leaning away from you. Support the front of his body with an open hand, your

fingers splayed on his chest to
keep him from flopping forward.

‣ *Facedown.* Lay him across your
lap, his head on your knees,
turned to one side.

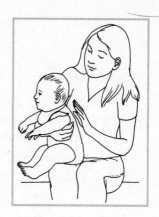

‣ *Over the shoulder.* Grasp him
under his arms, raise him to
a vertical position, and lean
him on and slightly over your
shoulder. Allow his legs to dangle
down, so that his body is in a
straight line.

In any of the above positions, use your free hand to rub his
back in a clockwise circular motion. You can also cup your hand
and gently pat his back to help move the gas bubble. In the facedown or over-the-shoulder position, use a "burp cloth"—a small
towel or diaper—under his head to protect your clothing if he
spits up.

WHAT IF . . . My Baby Spits Up?

Sometimes babies spit up—a small quantity of milk comes up with a burp. If this happens immediately after a feeding, your baby might be taking in more food than his little tummy can hold. If an hour or more has passed, spitting up more likely means he's swallowed air. When he burps, it expels the air, but milk and stomach fluids come up with it.

Spitting up is not the same as projectile vomiting, which is more dramatic, distressing to your baby, and sometimes caused by reflux. You can minimize her discomfort by burping her in the upright position. Wait at least twenty minutes before laying her down. It also helps to prop up the mattress with a towel or a blanket so that her head is slightly elevated. When you lay her down on her back, make sure that her face is turned to one side. That way, if she throws up, she won't choke on the secretion; it will come out of her mouth.

If she vomits while lying down, immediately lift her from the crib and blow air on her face, which makes her breathe faster and will clear her airway. Use a blue bulb aspirator to clear her mouth if necessary. If vomiting persists, especially accompanied by fever and/or diarrhea, consult your pediatrician.

Do I have to take special precautions with baby bottles? Whether you fill bottles with breast milk or formula, use extra care at first. Your newborn's immune system will not be fully developed until around his third month. But unless you live in a region where the drinking water is contaminated, you only have to sterilize your baby's bottles and nipples before the first use. After that, clean bottles in the dishwasher or hand-wash, using a long-handled bottle brush and dish soap.

A little common sense can help you avoid everyday germs. Always wash your hands before handling breast milk or mixing formula. Get in the habit of washing bottles out immediately. It will be easier to remove any milk residue. Air-dry bottles and nipples, covering them with a clean cloth or paper towel as a safeguard against airborne bacteria.

Breast milk can be refrigerated and rewarmed for the next feeding. However, never offer your baby a bottle of formula from which he's already drunk. Pumped breast milk can be stored in the refrigerator or freezer in bottles or bags designed especially for this purpose. You can mix a batch of formula, enough for a whole day, but do not keep it for more than twenty-four hours after it has been prepared.

The Sleepy Baby Problem

My clients are often appalled when I tell them they might have to wake their babies for feedings. Some newborns, regardless of whether they're formula-fed or breast-fed, sleep for hours during their first days, not even waking up to be fed. Their parents sometimes mistake them for "good babies." Others babies nurse for ten minutes or less and then fall asleep again. Both situations require waking.

Remember that your newborn spent nine months being fed by the umbilical cord. Now it is our job to teach him how to be on his own and to keep him going. We put a baby on her mother's breast as soon as she is born because that's when she is most alert. We know that in the days that follow, many babies turn into little sleepyheads. As a result, they eat less. Here's why it happens:

They're overwhelmed. In a week or so, your baby will have a stronger urge to eat, but in the beginning, it's hard for a newborn to be thrust into the world and to start breathing and eating on his own.

They're swaddled during feeding. While I always recommend swaddling for sleeping, it works against good feedings. Cozy babies tend to fall back to sleep.

They're given water. At this age, water is unnecessary. Breast milk and/or formula contain all the liquid your baby needs. If you give him water between feedings, his little tummy will already be partially full when it's time for a feeding. I wait six months before offering water, around the time we start solids.

They're not getting enough nutrition. A poorly fed baby becomes a tired baby. With breast-feeding, Mom's milk supply might be insufficient, or the baby is having trouble taking it in. With formula-feeding, it might be a matter of improper preparation—diluted formula with more water than the instructions call for. Whether this is done by accident or in an attempt to save money, changing the composition of formula in this way can make your baby weak and, therefore, more likely to fall asleep.

Sleeping through feedings or dozing off in the midst of a feeding, regardless of the cause, is a critical issue now for both of you, especially if you're breast-feeding. Every time your baby nurses, the sucking sends a message to your brain: make more milk. Not only does she take in less if she doesn't eat as often, but your body will also begin to manufacture less breast milk.

So if your formula-fed baby sleeps more than three and a half hours at a stretch or your breast-fed baby sleeps more than three hours, you must wake her. And if she falls asleep before she's taken in a sufficient amount of breast milk or formula, you must wake her.

I know, I know. You are absolutely horrified at the thought of disturbing your newborn's sleep. I've actually had mothers say that waking a sleeping baby is "cruel." But if you don't wake her, she will get used to eating small amounts at a time and become a "snacker," a baby who feeds for, say, ten minutes, falls asleep for a half hour, and then wakes up hungry. At worst, snackers eat every hour, night and day. Snacking is very difficult to reverse. And it can be the cause of sleep problems—yours and your baby's—in the weeks to come.

To my mind, what's really "cruel" is to make your baby go through suffering that could have been avoided. If your newborn falls asleep during a feeding, try one or more of the following strategies to keep him awake and coax him into having a full feeding:

› Burp him in an upright position.

› Change his diaper mid-feeding. Babies at this age can poop a few times between feedings. If he falls asleep, to wake him lay him on his back, remove his diaper, and clean him.

› If you're breast-feeding, use the football hold for better control of the baby's head, which makes it easier to help him latch on. If you're formula-feeding, check the manufacturer's directions to make sure you're preparing the bottles correctly.

› Remove all blankets, and, if necessary, take off her clothes, and feed her in her diaper. A warm, comfortable baby tends to go back to sleep.

› Lay her down on her back. Her legs and arms will start to twitch until she wakes up. Tickle her feet if not.

› Don't try to keep her awake by bouncing or swinging her— it will have the opposite effect.

› Moisten a soft towel with tepid (room temperature) water, and gently wipe it across her face and forehead until she awakens. Repeat if needed.

If your baby has slept more than three hours since his last feeding, and it's difficult to wake him, wait another thirty minutes. If you give him that extra time asleep, he might eat more, making up for the longer time between feedings. When you wake him again, remove his swaddling and lay him on his back. His legs and arms will start to twitch until he wakes up. Newborns do not like this position, so he's also likely to wake up crying, but at least he'll be awake.

Trust me, if you take these steps now, you'll only have to be this vigilant about your baby's sleeping for a few days, until she becomes more alert and stronger. She'll get better at sucking, too, diminishing the time it takes her to drain a bottle or a breast. If you don't, you'll be setting up a bad pattern of too-short feedings.

By the way, waking your baby is also an opportunity to witness how he makes the transition from sleep to consciousness. Some infants will just open their eyes and look around if you rouse them. Left to awaken on their own in their cribs, these babies tend not to cry, and if you don't rush in, they wait for you to come in. Others let you know loud and clear that you've disturbed them. They tend to be babies who, when they wake on their own, immediately start crying. In part, the difference is temperament. But it also depends on how *you* respond.

If You Feed Your Baby Formula

Formula is actually cow's milk that has been modified to be comparable to breast milk. Although there are minor differences between brands, most deliver a perfect balance of carbohydrates, proteins, and fats. In the United States, manufacturers are monitored for both quality and lead or pesticide contamination. Typically, brands are available in conventional or organic varieties and usually come in three forms (from most expensive to least): ready-made, concentrated liquid, and powder.

How do I choose a formula? Start with a cow-milk-based formula, such as Gerber's Good Start, which I frequently recommend. In my experience, it is the most gentle and has the least potential for allergic or gastrointestinal reaction. Often, the first formula you try is it—your baby has no skin reactions, has no diarrhea or gas, and starts regaining his birth weight. But if he doesn't react well to the first brand you try, talk to your pediatrician before switching to a new one. The formula you select will be your baby's sole source of nutrition until he's six months old and his main source of protein until he turns one. It's worth a bit of trial and error.

If I have to switch formulas, I start in the morning and do it gradually, in case the baby is allergic to the new one. For example, if the baby takes three ounces, start by giving him two ounces of the old one and, in another bottle, give him one ounce of the new one. With each feeding, increase the amount of the new formula. You might ask, "But Luiza, don't the two types mix in his stomach?" Yes, but that's the way I do it—it allows me better control over how much of the old and the new the baby ingests.

If your baby cries inconsolably after meals, has gas, spits up, or vomits frequently, it might mean that his sensitive digestive system is intolerant of one of the ingredients in the particular brand of formula he's ingesting. Your pediatrician might suspect lactose intolerance, a condition that plagues 1 to 3 percent of babies. Switching to a lactose-free formula might help. However, it's not always a matter of digestive issues. Fussy babies cry for different reasons, and a clear diagnosis is difficult, even for an experienced caregiver or medical professional. Sometimes the best you can do with a crying baby who can't get to sleep is to swaddle him and walk him around the house. You can also use a kangaroo-style baby carrier if you have one. Being close to your body might help him sleep.

What do I need to know about preparing formula? If the formula you choose comes in a can, devote one can opener exclusively to opening the containers. Before opening a can, always wipe the top with a paper towel or a clean, dry cloth. Once a can of liquid is open, you can refrigerate the unused portion in the same container, as long as you finish it before its expiration date.

Whether you use a liquid concentrate or powdered version, follow the instructions precisely. With the powdered version, measure only with the scoop that comes inside the container. If the directions call for a "level scoop," fill the scoop with powder, but don't tamp it down or bang it on the counter to cram in more. Simply scrape off any excess by swiping a knife (or a clean index finger) across the top, the same way you'd measure flour.

As with the liquid concentrate, take care to pour exactly the amount called for into a clean baby bottle. Making formula stronger to "bulk up" your baby could overload her digestive system and kidneys and cause dehydration. Skimping on the amount specified might stretch your dollar but lessen the nutritional value—and cause her to fall asleep on the job.

Concentrated liquid or powdered formula must be mixed with water. Tap water is fine in most places in the United States, especially in big cities where the water is treated. However, if the plumbing in your house is old, be on the cautious side. Never use hot water in formula, because it tends to contain more copper residue from old pipes. Instead, allow the cold water to run a few minutes. Most moms I know feel more secure using cold filtered water.

If you live in a small community or a rural area or your house is served by well water, you might want to inquire about the quality of your water supply. Bacterial contamination in small amounts can be tolerated by a healthy adult, but it is harmful to a newborn, until at least three months of age. So if you even suspect that your water supply could be low quality or contaminated, use bottled water, or boil your tap water before mixing it with your baby's formula. Two minutes is enough to kill harmful organisms and short enough to avoid a higher concentration of mineral impurities—the result of overboiling.

Should I prepare single bottles or batches of formula? Because formula is so easy to use, I advise preparing bottles as needed, rather than storing up "batches" of it that might go to waste. I start out making a two-ounce bottle. Once I see that the baby drinks at least that much, I increase the amount—by one ounce if the baby's on liquid formula, by two ounces if she's on powdered formula. That's because most powdered formulas call for one scoop per two ounces of water. It's easier—and safer—to make four-ounce bottles (requiring two scoops). If your baby doesn't finish, discard what's left. Whereas breast milk can be reused (only once) if kept in the refrigerator, leftover formula can't be reused. She'll work her way up to four ounces soon enough!

If, for convenience's sake, you want to have multiple bottles of formula on hand, never prepare more than you need for one day and night. Immediately refrigerate the extras. After that twenty-four-hour period, however, you should discard the unused formula and make a fresh batch.

What's the best way to warm a bottle? To warm a bottle you've retrieved from the refrigerator or if you prepare a bottle using cold water, heat a small pot of water to a temperature that allows you to comfortably dip your finger into it. Remove the pot from the stove. Place the bottle in the water for several minutes, until the formula is warm. Test it on the inside of your wrist. It should feel lukewarm. Use it right away. Don't reheat formula. Never microwave formula, because it will heat unevenly and, worst-case scenario, can burn your baby's mouth.

Chapter 7

IF YOU BREAST-FEED

Most newborns who weigh seven pounds or more when they're born are strong enough to nurse well, and most women in good health produce enough breast milk to sustain their babies. However, no one can anticipate whether a new mom will have trouble nursing or whether her baby will have trouble latching on and sucking. Some women, like Natalia, a client of mine, are afraid of breast-feeding at first because they've heard the horror stories. But at my urging, Natalia agreed at least to try to breast-feed. She watched in awe as I placed little Mica on her chest. He immediately searched for her breast. I explained that he was "rooting"—that's what newborns do—but she felt deep inside that Mica wanted *her*. At that moment, Natalia's decision was made.

For all the Natalias I've met, I also see women quit breast-feeding as early as the first month, which is long before the six-month mark recommended by the American Academy of Pediatrics. A 2007 survey by the Centers for Disease Control showed that while 75 percent of women nurse their babies in the hospital, only 33 percent are still exclusively breast-feeding at three months. They quit most often because breast-feeding is painful or too time-consuming or because they return to work and can't or don't want to pump. If a new mother has no support and problems develop as early as the first ten days, it then becomes a vicious cycle. The woman is exhausted, anxious, and in pain. She starts looking for any excuse to stop, which really is her way of saying, *This is just too hard.*

It doesn't have to be like that . . . *if* you develop good habits right from the beginning.

A Good "Latch"

Over the next week or so, when nutrition is critical for your baby and breast-feeding is still new for both of you, it's important to nurse frequently. Depending on your body and your baby, it can take from two to four days—at worst and in rare cases, five days—for your milk to begin flowing. However, I'd never let it go that long. When we are dealing with newborns, every hour counts.

All newborns get tired easily, but breast-fed babies are more prone to the "sleepy baby problem," because they have to work extra hard to extract milk, and that uses up a lot of energy. *You* have to work hard now, too, to make sure your baby is getting enough.

Feed her whenever she's hungry, "on demand." Wake her to feed her if she sleeps more than three hours. She needs to regain her birth weight. She needs the sucking practice. And she needs her strength, which good nutrition helps to build. Just as important, frequent nursing also stimulates your milk production. That's why it's so important, until your milk supply is established, to encourage your baby to nurse as much as possible.

Learning how to position your baby's mouth solidly on your nipple and at least half of your areola—the dark area surrounding the nipple—is one of the keys to successful breast-feeding. When

BREAST-FEEDING 101: THE FIRST FIVE DAYS

While your baby is nursing, pay attention. Is he sucking steadily? Does he swallow? Even before your milk comes in, your breasts will produce a small quantity of colostrum, which is a clear liquid. However, if several days go by, colostrum alone is not enough. Be aware of changes in your baby during these first few days. If he was alert and active when he came home from the hospital, has he become increasingly lethargic? If so, it might mean that your milk is coming in too slowly and that he's not getting proper nutrition. The small quantity of urine he excretes will be dark. You also might find orange-red crystals—a mix of calcium and urine—in his diaper. Either can mean that your baby is dehydrated. At that point, if not before, call your pediatrician. The doctor might advise you to hire a lactation nurse to monitor the baby. Some resist the idea of supplementing with formula, because bottle-feeding is typically not advised until breast-feeding is well established. But your baby has to eat—he can't wait until your milk comes in.

a baby sucks only the tip of the nipple, he can't extract much milk. It also makes your nipples sore, which can make breast-feeding very uncomfortable. Although mothers are typically given instruction in the hospital by a maternity nurse or lactation consultant, in my experience many come home needing additional help. I've seen situations in which just one bad latch-on damaged the mother's nipple, took weeks to heal, and made it difficult for the mother to keep nursing. (Special cases, such as when a baby is premature, is born with low weight, or has other physical complications that make it difficult or impossible to latch on, are beyond the scope of this book and require the help of a pediatrician and possibly a lactation consultant, who will work with you to decide what is best for your baby.)

Unless your baby has problems sucking, a proper latch-on almost guarantees proper nutrition. It also stimulates the production of hormones that cause your uterus to contract after childbirth, allowing it to return to its prepregnancy state. Giving your baby a good start will also relax *you* and build your confidence.

If your baby is latched on improperly, it's better to take her off your breast and start over. Interrupt the feeding by placing your finger in the corner of her mouth and gently pulling it sideways, releasing the pressure. Then try again.

Don't get discouraged. At first, many newborns have trouble finding or staying on Mom's breast. Some get so frustrated they can't latch on. Or they might appear to be latched on but aren't really swallowing. This is why it's especially important during these first days of breast-feeding to pay close attention. In my experience, most babies eventually get the hang of it and become proficient breast-feeders. Don't panic if your baby doesn't immediately latch on. I have a few tricks that can make it easier:

› First, squeeze a drop of breast milk, water, or formula onto your nipple. Having something to swallow will help calm your baby, and he will start to suck.

› Gently guide him back toward your breast, placing your thumb and fingers around your areola. Once your baby masters the art of breast-feeding, you won't need to hold your breast while he's nursing,

› Tickle his lips with your nipple until he opens his mouth. Help him get his entire mouth around your nipple and at least half of your areola by placing his head against your breast.

▸ Once your baby's mouth begins to close over your areola, pull his chin down with your free hand, coaxing him into the correct position. His mouth should cover almost the entire areola, not just the nipple, and his nose should be facing your nipple.

If your baby is latched on properly, he will probably suck a few times before swallowing. You'll be able to hear him swallow. Once he gets started, he will pause a few seconds to breathe and then keep sucking and swallowing until he's satisfied.

WHAT IF . . . My Baby Latches On Properly but Still Seems to Have Trouble Sucking?

Some babies latch on successfully but still do not nurse properly. Sometimes it's because Mom doesn't produce enough milk, and the baby, tired from sucking so hard, either cries out of frustration or is so exhausted he falls asleep while eating. But some babies also have sucking problems as early as a few hours after birth. They might roll their tongues, or they're too weak to suck.

In her first feeds, did your baby move her cheeks and make noise but really only suck with her tongue? If she doesn't pull in the entire nipple when she sucks, she can only get milk that drips from your nipple, which won't be enough. Babies can also develop this problem if they lose as much as a pound in the first ten days, which is considered significant weight loss.

Whether a sucking problem is evident immediately or happens later, it can prevent your baby from getting adequate nutrition. If your newborn is unable to suck correctly for a period of twenty-four hours (even with your help), call your pediatrician. In the meantime, try these steps:

- If it appears that she is having trouble getting milk from your breast, and you're sure you have a proper latch-on, take her off your breast, and wait until she opens her mouth wider. What does her tongue look like? If it bends toward the roof of her mouth, lower it with your index finger. Gently pressing her chin downward toward her chest will also help bring her tongue down.

- Make another attempt to breast-feed, and even though she's not getting enough of your milk, allow her to suck for ten minutes. After that, you can put your pinkie in her mouth, which also gives her sucking practice. Some babies give up sucking when extracting milk from their mother is difficult.

- When your baby has finished sucking, extract your milk using a manual or electric pump.

- Finish the feeding by using a bottle, dropper, or syringe to give her the breast milk you pumped. Normally, I don't suggest giving a bottle to a baby who's learning to breast-feed, but the most important consideration at this point is nutrition. We must keep feeding her while we work on solving the problem. If your body is not manufacturing any or enough breast milk at this point, your pediatrician will probably suggest supplementing with formula rather than deprive your baby.

- Continue using this technique for the next twenty-four to seventy-two hours, which is usually how long it takes to correct the problem. As your baby becomes fortified, she will ingest larger amounts, become stronger, and be able to suck more efficiently.

One Breast at a Time

Your breasts actually produce three different kinds of milk. First, however, your breasts produce *colostrum*, the perfect food for your newborn. It contains white blood cells and antibodies that protect your baby from infections while simultaneously forming a protective layer in her intestines. Because of its high protein content and low sugar, colostrum prepares her digestive system for your milk and facilitates digestion. Colostrum also helps stimulate your baby's first bowel movement, which consists of a dark green substance, meconium. Your breast-fed baby can extract only a small amount of colostrum at each feed, so she has to eat more often until your milk begins to come in.

Once your milk starts to flow, during each feeding, your breasts will release the thin *fore milk*, which looks like a bluish skim milk, followed by the thicker, creamier, fat-rich *hind milk*. By emptying one breast fully, your baby gets both kinds of milk, and you can be certain that he's getting all the nutrients he needs. If he drains one breast during a feeding (unlikely in the first ten days), only then would you switch breasts.

At first, nursing your baby can take as long as forty-five minutes. But as I said earlier, when your milk is just beginning to come in, don't watch the clock. If your newborn is latched on and sucking properly, limiting the time of feeding can frustrate him and reduce your milk supply.

If your baby just "snacks"—takes a little milk and falls asleep—she will never get to the valuable hind milk. Plus, her erratic suckling will send a message to your body telling your mammary glands not to produce as much milk. However, babies who latch on properly don't usually become snackers. So pay attention in these first few days. Make sure that your baby is sucking *and* swallowing. Try to wake her when she falls asleep on the job.

Trust me, being careful now will be a lot easier than trying to fix the problem later.

If your baby doesn't last long between feedings at first—say, every one and a half to two hours—it's absolutely essential to alternate breasts. Don't be afraid that the unused breast will get too full. You're going to be nursing him practically around the clock this week, and by alternating breasts, you can be sure that both will be emptied.

Of course, things don't always go as planned. Monica, for example, gave birth to Justin, a healthy six-pound, three-ounce boy who was a vigorous eater from the beginning. But Monica's body wasn't producing enough milk. Justin worked hard to extract even that little bit of milk, but he didn't get enough nutrition to replace the calories he spent on sucking. When he started to lose weight, we were concerned.

So I adjusted his feeding schedule for more frequent feedings—every three hours around the clock, ten minutes on each breast. Immediately after a feeding, Monica would use a powerful electric pump for five minutes to empty both breasts. I then gave him the pumped milk to finish his feeding. We repeated the process around the clock for about one week until Justin started to gain weight.

You might wonder why we put Justin on Monica's breast when not much milk was available. There were two reasons. Babies like to suck, and even when they're good at it, they need to keep practicing. Just as important, sucking stimulates the flow of breast milk. Whenever your baby suckles, your breasts send a message to your body: *Keep the milk coming—we have a hungry baby here!*

Frequent feedings during these first ten days also help prevent your breasts from becoming engorged—hard, swollen, uncomfortably full, even painful—which can happen when breasts aren't drained properly. Once your milk starts flowing, you can relax and spread feedings as much as three hours apart. If you have a large baby with a voracious appetite who can go three hours between feedings almost from the beginning, nurse him on one side, but also pump the other breast, so it also empties.

Breast-Feeding Positions

Many mothers ask, "What's the best way to hold my baby when breast-feeding?"

The answer depends on your body—and your baby. You have several options. But in each case, you will hold the baby with one hand or arm and your breast with the other. Especially if you are big-breasted, give yourself extra support by placing four fingers on one side of your breast and your thumb on the other, at around the nine o'clock and three o'clock positions.

For all but the belly-to-belly position (see below), a comfortable chair with armrests is best. Have several pillows on hand to support your back and the arm holding the baby. It's also good to have a stool or an extra pillow for your feet if they don't reach the floor. Nestling the two of you in pillows will make you more relaxed and your baby more comfortable. Experiment to find out what feels best. Some women buy "donuts" or "Boppys"—special pillows designed for nursing—but I think bed pillows do the job just as well.

AFTER A C-SECTION, WHAT'S THE BEST POSITION?

There's no such thing as a "best" feeding position. But if you've had a cesarean and have been told to stay in a reclining position, or if it's hard for you to sit, try the belly-to-belly position first. I also recommend the football hold when a mother cannot support the baby in her lap. If you use one of the other sitting positions, at least put your baby on a pillow (or two), which will avoid putting too much pressure directly on your incision.

Although most lactating women's breasts "tell" them which breast was given last—the unused breast feels full—if you're new to breast-feeding, keep track. Have a notepad by your nursing chair, or use a safety pin or clip on your clothing as a reminder of which breast you last used. Each of the descriptions below assumes that you are feeding from the right breast. (Substitute "left" for "right" if you are offering your left breast.)

Classic Position

This is also called the cradle position, because your baby's head is nestled—cradled—in the crook of your right arm. Position him in your lap (or on a pillow) so that he's lying on his left side, horizontally or at a slight incline, his head a bit higher than his

feet. His whole body should be facing your breast. Tuck his left (bottom) arm under your right arm. It might help to put your feet on a stool or a foot rest, so that you're not stretching down toward him. This is often the position of choice if you've had a vaginal birth and the baby has had no difficulties with latch-on. It is also used by mothers who bottle-feed.

Cross Hold

A reverse of the classic or cradle position. Instead of supporting your baby's head in the crook of your right arm, use your left hand and arm to hold him. This is sometimes a better alternative for a small baby or one who has trouble latching on, because you have greater control of his head.

Football Hold

Place your baby on a pillow at your right side so that she is on her left side, resting on your right arm, with her feet pointing toward your back. Support her head with your right hand, as if you're carrying a football. It's helpful to gently place the thumb of your right hand on her right ear and your index finger on her left ear, so that you can better control her head, neck, and shoulders. It's good for mothers who have flat nipples or babies who have trouble latching on, because you have greater control of your baby's head. If you have large

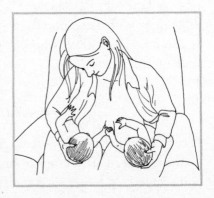

breasts, it's easier to see what you're doing. Sometimes mothers of twins also prefer this position, because they can feed both babies at the same time.

Belly-to-Belly

You both will be lying down, facing each other—you on your right side, the baby on his left. Use a pillow to support his back so that he cannot accidentally roll backward. You can also put a pillow under your head and shoulders and one between your slightly bent knees. Experiment and figure out what feels best. Gently hold your baby's head with your right hand, and touch his lips with the tip of your nipple. It will activate his sucking reflex, and he'll open his mouth. When his mouth is wide open, push his head toward your breast. If your baby seems to have trouble reaching your breast, boost him up a bit by placing a folded receiving blanket under his head. That way, he's at your level, and he might not have to strain to reach your nipple. Assuming that you and your baby do well in this position, it's also the least disruptive when breast-feeding in the middle of the night.

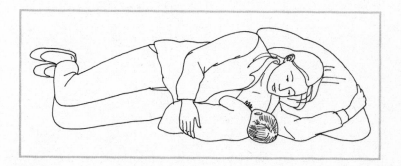

HOW TO TELL WHEN IT'S GOING WELL

The following guidelines can tell you whether your breast-fed baby is getting adequate nutrition in the first ten days. If she shows any of the signs in the right column, it's time to consult your pediatrician:

You're on the right breast-feeding path if (after ten days) . . .

+ Her urine is clear.
+ She sucks rhythmically, and you can hear her swallow when she's nursing.
+ When she's awake, she reacts to the sound of your voice and looks at moving objects.
+ She sleeps two hours between feedings.
+ She wets 5 to 7 diapers (some very heavily) within a 24-hour period.

Your baby might not be feeding well if . . .

+ She has little or no urine in her diapers over a 24-hour period.
+ Her urine is bright yellow and very concentrated; you might also see crystals in her diaper.
+ Her suction is weak, and you can't hear her swallow when she's nursing.
+ She doesn't seem alert when awake and is slow to respond to stimulation.
+ She doesn't sleep between feedings and always seems to be hungry.

Taking Care of Your Breasts

Breast-feeding can be physically uncomfortable in the beginning. You can minimize the discomfort and avoid more serious problems by heeding my advice. Start on day one. Take the steps below. This may sound like hard work, but if you take the time now, you won't have to do it for long. Once your milk is flowing and your baby has learned how to suck, you can relax and let Mother Nature take over:

- Before each feeding, place a warm compress on your breasts. This will make your let-down easier and help soften any hardness before it gets worse.

- Take a daily bath—or several, if necessary—to relax yourself and keep your skin clean. Do not use soap or soap products on your breasts. Soap interferes with the natural oil that keeps the skin lubricated around the nipple. If you have large breasts, you'll notice that you breasts weigh even more now than they did in pregnancy. Even if you have smaller breasts, you will also feel "full." And no matter how big your breasts are, they can sometimes feel rock-hard. This condition is temporary, mostly in the first twenty-four to forty-eight hours, but because some women are not taught how to care for their breasts and nipples, this hardness can last longer and cause additional problems.

- Wear a bra that provides good supports for your breasts. Most maternity shops carry good nursing bras and can show you the difference between various styles.

- Make your baby suck whenever he is awake. Frequent feedings this week make it less likely that your breasts will become engorged or at least will help you avoid a severe case of engorgement.

- Make sure that your baby is latched on correctly.

- After feeding, squeeze your nipple to extract a drop of colostrum or, if it has already started to flow, milk. With your fingers, spread the liquid on your nipples and let it dry before closing your bra. This will prevent irritation and cracks.

> ‣ Place a warm compress over your breast after feeding, too, and keep it there until it gets cool. A moistened disposable diaper, microwaved for twenty to thirty seconds, works best. The diaper holds the heat longer than a wet towel and is less of a mess. You can even place it on your bra or shirt without worrying about getting wet.

> ‣ Between feedings, massage your breasts in a circular motion. If you come across a hard spot, or "knot," use a hot compress on that spot, and knead the area gently with your fingers.

> ‣ Alternate breast-feeding positions. If you always nurse your baby in the same position, milk can build up in certain areas of the breast, which is how hard spots form. The football hold and the cross hold, which make it easier to control your baby's head, also help extract milk from all areas of the breast.

Naturally, lactating patterns vary widely among women. You might produce very little milk initially, and the more your baby sucks, the more your output will increase. Or you might produce a large volume of milk immediately.

WHAT IF . . . It's Painful?

It's normal to have a little sensitivity and soreness when you first begin to breast-feed, but breast-feeding shouldn't hurt. Problems can start on the very first feeding. If your baby sucks only on the tip of your nipple or begins to chew on your nipple, it will hurt and take a long time to heal, turning breast-feeding into a painful matter. Your body is "telling" you . . .

Take better care of your breasts and nipples. Review the guidelines for breast care above. Also, instead of having the baby nurse directly, protect your nipples with a silicone nipple shield. Use a silicone nipple protector in your bra, too, so that the fabric doesn't chafe your sore nipples.

Your breasts are engorged. This can happen if you don't nurse your baby frequently enough in the first few days after birth. Your breasts might feel hard, lumpy, uncomfortably full—or they can swell to the point where the areola hardens and the nipples "disappear." Here, too, a warm compress on your breasts or a warm tub will ease the pressure. You might also have to empty your breasts a little by pumping *before* each feeding.

Your baby is not well positioned on your breast. Don't grin and bear it. At the first sign of discomfort, interrupt the feeding by easing your pinkie into the corner of your baby's mouth and gently pulling it sideways, releasing him from your nipple. Review the steps to a proper latch-on, and then try again. It's also helpful to change to a belly-to-belly position or a football hold, which allows you better control of his head. Tease his mouth open with your nipple, and then use your free hand to push his head toward your breast.

Remember, too, that painful feedings often indicate that your baby isn't getting enough to eat, which always warrants a call to your pediatrician. Perhaps you need a lactation consultant, too, someone who can sit with you as you feed your baby, help you with the latch-on, and figure out whether a particular position might work better.

Supplementing with Formula

Some new mothers don't produce enough breast milk to nourish their babies. The solution is to supplement with formula. Below are the most common reasons that breast-feeding might be difficult or impossible.

Low birth weight. Babies less than six pounds generally have a weaker sucking reflex.

Immediate breast-feeding difficulties. Although it sometimes takes a few feedings to get a baby to latch on and suck, some pediatricians will insist that you immediately supplement with formula. Mom, this doesn't mean that your baby will be "on" formula. It's just an aid to give your baby proper nutrition and keep him going *until* your milk comes in.

Weak or improper sucking. As I noted earlier, some babies can latch on but are too weak to suck long enough for a proper feeding. Others do not nurse properly—they move their cheeks and make noise but really only suck with their tongues—and are therefore unable to grasp the entire nipple. They only take in whatever drips from the nipples, which isn't enough breast milk to sustain them.

Prematurity. Babies born at thirty-six weeks or earlier (more than three weeks before the due date) generally do not have the strength to breast-feed.

◆ ◆ ◆

When I started working as a baby nurse in the 1960s, formula was as popular as breast milk is today. All the babies I cared for were on it. Formula is still an excellent source of nutrition for your baby. Also, as I pointed out earlier, breast-feeding is only a small part of taking care of your newborn. If your doctor or your lactation specialist concludes that your breasts are not producing enough milk, it's fine to switch to formula, because it's a good nutritional substitute for breast milk.

However, if your baby weighs at least six pounds and you are producing *some* milk, even though it's not enough to satisfy her fully, go to the breast first, not the bottle, so that her sucking stimulates your milk production. Feed her in her diaper only, which will keep her awake and give her sucking practice. If she seems hungry afterward, offer formula, too. However, all babies are satisfied after having some formula, so if yours continues to be fussy, it could be that she is tired or she ate too fast and is having some tummy discomfort. Swaddling will help calm her.

The concern about switching back and forth between breast milk and formula is that the baby might learn to prefer formula but not because of any difference in taste. Babies at this age can't taste the difference between breast milk and formula. Sucking on a bottle is easier than extracting milk from your breast, because the silicone nipple allows the liquid to drip into her mouth without much effort on her part. Because she has to suck harder on your flesh nipple, she might refuse it altogether. Here's what I suggest to help prevent your baby from giving up:

› Experiment with different kinds of nipples to see what works best with your baby. I usually suggest starting with one that looks most like your own nipple and has the slowest flow. Although a slow-flow nipple won't work exactly like your breast, it at least makes her suck a little harder.

› After a bottle-feeding, delay the breast-feeding as long as possible. Remember that formula takes longer to digest, so your baby might last up to an hour longer after a formula feeding. More important, the hungrier your baby is, the more likely it is that he'll be willing to work at extracting milk from your nipple.

› After two unsuccessful breast-feedings, use an electric
   pump to empty your breasts. Store the yield in a bottle, and
   give it to your baby at his next feeding.

Be patient. Don't give up too quickly. Sometimes the first days
seem to be impossible. How to get through them? Your baby's
crying; you're in pain. Initially, it will seem easier to you, too, to
offer your baby a bottle than to attempt breast-feeding again. But
try to stay calm. This phase will pass. Switching back and forth
between bottle and breast is tricky with an infant who is ten days
old or younger, but once your milk is established and you get over
this hurdle, breast-feeding will become easier and, in my opinion,
is well worth the effort.

Chapter 8

PROTECTING YOUR NEWBORN: PRECAUTIONS AND RISKS

Your little one is a newcomer, just getting used to the world. Everything's strange and wide open. We need to keep her warm without overheating, and we need to protect her. To some infants, life outside the womb feels harsh. Depending on her temperament, your baby might fit right into the hubbub of your household, or it may take a while for her to get used to her new surroundings. Either way, it helps to be aware of how siblings, partners, pets, and visitors can affect this newest member of the family.

Room Temperature for Your Baby

Now that you have a little one in the house, choose a temperature that feels comfortable for you, but remember that your baby doesn't move much, because he spends a lot of his time asleep. For him, the house will feel a little colder than it does to you, especially when he's sleeping. Also, newborns lose temperature very fast when undressed, so keep that in mind when changing or cleaning him. My advice is to dress your newborn with one layer more than the clothing you are wearing. You should especially monitor the temperature in your baby's room, to make sure it's not too cool in the summer if you have air-conditioning. Typically, I tell clients to set their thermostats to around seventy-four degrees. For baths, I warm up the room or bathroom to around seventy-nine degrees.

But do not trust my numbers or your thermostat! Make adjustments based on your house, how your system works, and what's comfortable for the baby. Don't assume that one size fits all. Check on your baby to see if he is warm enough by touching his cheeks with the back of your hand. His hands and feet might feel cold, but his temperature is best tested by feeling his face. That will give you an idea if baby needs an extra layer of clothing, such as a onesie under her pajamas.

Basically, it's a matter of common sense. Keep your baby dressed warmer in cold weather—a onesie with a second layer over it—and more lightly when it's hot. If your home is air-conditioned, be mindful that temperatures can vary from room to room (so the thermostat for the whole house might not always be accurate for your baby's room).

Guarding Your Baby's "Space"

In the first ten days, I suggest staying close to home. If you take the baby out and weather permits, go to a place where you both can get some fresh air, not a mall or another crowded place. Of course, you might have crowds at home, too, once everyone hears the good news about your precious arrival.

Siblings

I believe that the birth of a new family member calls for a celebration. You don't have to change your lifestyle because of the new baby, but it will change everyone's life. If there are older siblings, I hope you have prepared them for the new arrival. Some children view the baby as an invader. Often, that's because their parents all but apologize to them for bringing home a sibling ("Oh, honey, don't worry, I still love you"). One little boy I knew gave his new sister such a hard time that sometimes I feared for her life.

Fortunately, most of my clients do the right thing. They talk about the new baby with the child and about all the fun things they'll do. They let the sibling choose some of the baby's clothing and toys. They make the child proud of his new status. They read books about becoming a big sister or brother.

Even though at times older siblings naturally feel some anger toward the new arrival, with their parents' help and attention they eventually realize that there's enough love to go around. Little by little, the older sibling bonds with the baby and becomes his most vocal supporter.

Visitors

Most new mothers understandably want to show off their babies. Many ask me, "Should I let visitors hold him?" I'd advise caution and common sense. Too much commotion can overwhelm a sensitive baby. If he stays up too long and gets overtired, he'll cry nonstop. Most important, your newborn's immune system isn't fully developed, so when he is exposed to a virus, he might not be able to fight it. Any kind of respiratory infection can interfere with his ability to swallow and breathe properly. Also, getting sick at such a young age will affect his eating and sleeping patterns. Breast-fed babies have some protections against illness, but even then, I wouldn't take a chance. Especially during cold and flu season, ask relatives or friends with stuffy noses or aches and pains to wait and visit once they feel better.

When I'm in a household, I always ask visitors to wash their hands and not to wear highly scented perfumes or lotions. Imagine it from your baby's perspective, having your nose on someone's skin or perfumed clothing, breathing in the strong smell. And what if the baby is allergic to something in the perfume?

Safe Space

You always have to be one step ahead to protect your baby's space. Providing a quiet, uncrowded environment during her first few weeks will help her adjust to the world outside the womb. Besides making sure that her crib and other equipment are safe, we also have to make sure that your baby is safe wherever you put her down. Here are some guidelines for crib and floor:

› Keep the area (especially around her face) clear of blankets, pillows, and toys.

› Any surface on which you lay your baby must be firm.

› Do not leave the baby in a room with a cigarette smoker or where there are strong odors, such as from cleaning products or nail polish.

Sometimes people ask, "Isn't it better for babies to get used to whatever is going on in the household?" My experience shows me that it depends on the baby. Some newborns will sleep no matter what, but others become cranky when they're overstimulated by loud noises and strong smells. If you think about it, adults relax and sleep better when their surroundings are calm. Why wouldn't babies?

WHAT IF . . . An Older Sibling Is Sick?

I worked in a household once where the baby, Zack, had two sisters, and the older one, five-year-old Patti, was fighting a cold. Patti was coughing a lot, but the pediatrician told the mother not to worry: Since she was breast-feeding, Zack had immunity. I was worried nonetheless, because the mom often fed Zack in Patti's room. Patti would play on the floor nearby and every now and then become curious about the baby, get close, and cough in Zack's face.

Then Zack started coughing, too. I paid attention to the color of his skin, his temperature, and his breathing. I was quite anxious, waiting for the first twenty-four hours to go by. His condition got worse. He had no fever, but that also worried me a bit. When fighting an infection, a higher-than-normal temperature is a sign that the body is fighting back. The pediatrician kept telling the mother not to worry—the baby would fight this infection, because he was getting his mother's milk. In all my years, I had never seen a one-week-old child with a bad cold. But I'm not a doctor. I had to take his word.

As it turned out, the pediatrician was wrong. Zack ended up in the hospital. What I learned from this was to trust myself and always to take the safer route. In *most* cases, pediatricians are right: breast milk protects a newborn. But obviously not always. Luckily, Zack recovered, and now it's all a distant memory.

But why take the chance? If a sibling is sick, no matter how much he or she wants to be with the new baby, it is better to delay their time together than to have a sick infant.

Bringing Baby Home to a Pet

The probability of a pet hurting a baby is greater than that of a pet hurting an adult (or the baby hurting the pet!). Here are some ways to keep your little one safe:

> When you're in the hospital, have your partner or a friend give your pet a blanket or a onesie that has your baby's scent on it.

> It takes three weeks or longer for a pet to adapt to a new baby. Yours might totally ignore the new addition or be intensely curious. Either way, *never* leave the two of them alone together.

> Even in your presence, try to avoid situations in which the animal might make sudden movements or unexpected noises, such as a loud bark.

> Keep the pet at a safe distance from your newborn, who could inadvertently grab a handful of fur, thanks to his grasp reflex.

> Pets are not very different from children! They also need to get used to new things in their environment. Treating pets with kindness and attention increases the likelihood that they will feel safe and comfortable around tiny humans.

> Vaccinate your animals, especially against rabies.

SIDS: What We Know, What We Can Do

In my early years as a baby nurse in Brazil, we put most babies on their tummies to sleep. When they woke in the middle of the night, most were able to go back to sleep after fussing for a few minutes. But during the last twenty years, as technology has made it easier to study babies, scientists began to ask why some infants died mysteriously in the night without apparent cause. They called it sudden infant death syndrome, or SIDS. In the early 1990s, when I started working as a baby nurse in the United States, the American Academy of Pediatrics recommended that all babies sleep face up as a precaution.

But what if a baby doesn't like to sleep on his back? Can he be put to sleep on his belly? Babies do not talk, and therefore it is difficult to know what they like. But some infants, mainly the most difficult-to-calm babies (which I talk about in chapter 15), tend to cry a lot and cry even more when placed on their backs. Lying on their tummies does, in fact, help them to sleep better and longer than lying in a face-up position.

So if babies seem to sleep better on their bellies, and generations of children were routinely put to sleep this way, can you make an exception if your baby has trouble settling down? My answer, as a professional working with babies all the time, is no. It's not worth the risk.

Babies who sleep on their stomachs are more inclined to suffer from apnea (a pause in breathing). They tend to breathe in the air they exhale, which can increase the levels of carbon dioxide in their bodies. Their temperatures also rise as a result of sleeping on their tummies. It is possible that some or all of these factors play a role in SIDS, but scientists still don't know what actually causes babies to die so suddenly. It has never been proven that sleeping on the tummy *causes* SIDS. However, babies who sleep on their stomachs are 13 percent more likely to die than babies who are put to sleep on their backs. Even more important, when the majority of families started to place babies on their backs in the '90s, SIDS became less common.

SIDS concerns me and causes new mothers nights of worry. One mother I know hired a baby nurse just to watch her infant sleep. How do *I* ease my anxiety? I put all my babies to sleep on their backs. (For more information, consult the American SIDS Institute website, http://sids.org.)

Notes on the First Ten Days

My Baby's Name—and How We Chose It

_____

_____

_____

Delivery Details

_____

_____

_____

Meeting My Baby

Weight? _____

Height? _____

Rituals/Ceremonies

_____

_____

_____

Visitors

_____

_____

_____

Gifts/Surprises

_____

_____

_____

Best Moments

_____

_____

_____

Worst Moments

_____

_____

_____

PHASE III

The First Month:
OMG, The Baby's Staying!

IN A NUTSHELL

This is when reality sets in. Our objective since the first days of life is to help babies develop good habits. But now we want to try to nudge them gently from "on demand" toward my "eat, play, sleep" routine: feedings move farther apart, your baby gets playtime after each feeding, and then, with a little cuddling and soothing, she sleeps.

COVERED IN THIS PHASE:

Start thinking about your routine

Eat: good feeding, good routine

Play: bathing and massage

Sleep: sending baby to dreamland

Who's taking care of *you*, Mom?

*C*an you believe your baby is a week old? If you listened to my advice, you're napping when she's napping. You're still tired, of course, because you're waking up several times during the night, and you're likely to be doing that for the next many weeks. To me, as a professional, this is the most tiring month. Newborns are nursed every one or two hours in the first week and, from then on, two or three hours around the clock. They take small portions during each feeding, take a break to sleep, and then they're hungry again, which makes Mom exhausted.

There's not much you can do about this except ride it out and begin to establish good habits. On a happier note, you're probably not quite as shocked as you were a week ago about being a mother and how much time and energy it requires. But it also depends on what kind of baby you have. If you have an easy baby, you've conquered the challenges of the first week, and there aren't many surprises. If not, you still might be working on those issues.

In either case, your job now is to be a detective and figure out what kind of little person your baby is—his nature, his reactions, what he likes and doesn't like. My job this month is to make sure you're at least starting to think about establishing a repeating and predictable pattern of care that will help both of you get through the day.

But Luiza, you might ask, *didn't you say that you have to follow the baby?* Yes! But I also say that it's easier to start good habits now, instead of having to change things later. Think of it as "newborn school." You are your child's most important teacher. I understand that with a new baby, making life consistent is easier to say than to do. However, if you begin now—if only to become aware of what it takes to gently nudge your baby into a routine—and you keep working toward your goal over these next few months, your baby will eventually eat, play, and sleep at regular intervals.

Some of my clients balk at first at these ideas. Many are busy, powerful people. The fathers work late. Typically, the mothers have waited until their thirties or forties to have babies. They are so happy to become mothers, they tell me, that they don't care if the baby falls asleep in their arms, nursing, rocking, and so on. They say they have to keep the babies up until their husbands get home from the office so that the dads get a chance to be with them. I always ask, are you aware of the consequences of those choices? Are you OK with having a baby who can only fall asleep if she's being held? Are you willing to pay the price of keeping her up late and having a cranky baby the next day? If you say yes, I'm OK, too. It's your baby and your family. However, if you think that you will be able to change those habits whenever you please, I warn you, it's not easy. Besides, why put your baby (and yourself) through the difficult process of reversing a behavior she has gotten used to?

Of course, this also depends on your baby's temperament, which will become more apparent as this month progresses. If you have an easy child, you'll have an easier first month. If you have a difficult-to-calm child, you're in for a challenge. But I can help. My "formula" is:

instinct + information + patience + love = a happy child.

I know firsthand that by starting now, we can, little by little, guide any baby to good habits if we think about routine. Having a plan will affect how your baby eats and sleeps, her hand and eye coordination, her cooing and smiling. We adults are happier when our lives are well planned and when we know what's coming next. So are babies.

Chapter 9

START THINKING ABOUT
YOUR ROUTINE

No one really knows how this story started, but many have retold it. A new commander was put in charge of an air force base in Brazil. While he was reviewing basic procedures, the commander was puzzled to see a guard standing next to a cement embankment. All the other sentries were at exits and other secure areas. What was this man guarding, a pile of concrete? After asking several officers, he found out. The previous commander had placed a man there because, at the time, the area had been freshly cemented, and they didn't want trespassers. And although the embankment had long since dried properly, no one had thought to ask why a guard should be assigned such a useless task.

I share this story because whether it's a military headquarters or a home with a new baby, a routine should not exist for routine's sake. We must continually ask, "What purpose does it serve?" And as time goes on, "Is it still working?" or "Do we need to adjust it?"

Why Do We Need a Routine at All?

Many mothers are confused by the term "routine." Some even hate the idea of a routine. To them, it means repetition, tedious work, a lack of excitement in their everyday lives. They're also afraid it will tie them down. The problem is, they don't understand what a routine is supposed to do.

If there's nothing else you take away from this book, above all is the importance of establishing a routine that works for you, one that is based on your child's age, temperament, and needs. Instead of worrying about how a routine might restrict you, take my word for it, it won't. It will eventually give you *more* freedom.

We don't have a routine for routine's sake. I urge you to establish a routine for several reasons:

> ‣ A routine imposes order in your baby's world and is the best way of ensuring that his needs will be met. He has arrived in a strange world that he can't begin to understand yet.

> ‣ A routine strengthens the maternal bond, because it helps develop trust. An unspoken communication starts to develop between you and your baby. She starts to know your movements and what to expect.

> ‣ Your baby will thrive and respond better to everything in her environment when life is predictable. We are all creatures of habit. When life is in order, we feel good and safe.

> ‣ Others can take care of your baby—Dad, a professional, your mom—without your having to worry about whether he's getting what he needs.

Let me be very clear, even though I am repeating myself. During the first month, I don't "schedule" a baby. I start by following *the baby*. At the same time, though, I do try to bring order to his day, establish a pattern of care. That's not only good for the baby, but it's also good for the household. Someone else will have to care for that baby on my days off and long after I'm gone from that household. With a good routine, the baby will be taken care of in a way that he's used to, even when I'm not in charge. A mother who goes back to work after the baby is born (or a mom who wants time for herself) is the primary caretaker, but she, too, will have to delegate caretaking to a relative or a professional.

This doesn't happen overnight. It only happens when we keep reinforcing the same behaviors over and over. With baby Luigi, as I do with all of my babies, I consistently followed the eat-play-sleep pattern. The first week, I fed and burped him. Luigi, of course, didn't "play" then, but after a feeding, I'd carry him around or talk to him for a few minutes. Then I would swaddle him and put him into his bassinet. Some days, he went right off to sleep; on others, he needed a little comforting. Even though newborns change every day, we stuck with the eat-play-sleep pattern.

There are, of course, times when your everyday pattern is disrupted by something out of the ordinary—a family outing or travel, for example. But it's important to get back to normal as soon as possible. Some babies will protest a bit if they've gotten used to a new regimen—maybe Grandpa kept him up later—but be firm. A baby who has been "taught" well in "newborn school" will get back to the eat-play-sleep routine with minimal help.

By the time Luigi was a month old, he could stay up around thirty minutes after a feeding. I'd put him under his Gymini or in the infant seat. At the first sign of fatigue—a yawn, a little cry—I'd swaddle him and put him to bed. As in the first week, there were days when he cried before falling asleep. I'd burp him or perhaps walk around a little until his discomfort subsided. He wasn't yet on a routine, but every day, we were inching toward it. At first, it was sometimes challenging to get him to nap for more than thirty to forty-five minutes, especially in the afternoon when he really needed it. Many one-month-olds tend to take too-short naps. So until Luigi was able to sleep for longer stretches, to help him stay asleep, I'd put him on my chest and get some needed rest myself.

I'll talk specifically about how to lay a foundation for each part of eat-play-sleep in the next few chapters. But I tell you about Luigi now because I want you to know that having a routine works. By the time Luigi was six months old, he was waking at seven A.M., eating five to six times a day—mostly breast milk and a little solid food—having two or three hours of play between feedings, and taking good morning and afternoon naps, always at pretty much the same times. He was a good sleeper at night, too. Routine was his friend.

Your baby's routine will involve trial and error at first, and it will change as she changes. Remember that the way to do things is little by little, until we get them right. You won't get your routine right all the time. But tomorrow is another day.

Let Your Routine Guide You

Having a predictable routine is, in part, about executing the everyday chores of childcare—feeding, diapering, dressing, bathing, and sleeping rituals. Those are just tasks. They don't necessarily convey love. But if you do them with patience, openness, and attentiveness, your everyday routine becomes more than just a series of repeated activities. Each chore can be viewed as another opportunity to study your baby's behavior and adjust what you're doing based on your own baby, not on what other mothers do. By observing your baby throughout the day—how he takes to feedings, what positions he prefers, his sleep patterns, his reactions to strangers and unfamiliar places—you know what matters. You'll know what to do, because you've been paying attention.

This is vitally important in the first few weeks as you become acquainted with the unique sounds and gestures that your baby makes to "tell" you what he needs. When every day has a particular pattern, it's easier to be a detective. For example, cries aren't always about hunger. When your baby cries, she also might be overtired or cold. How do you tell the difference? By being aware of your infant's routine. When something doesn't go as planned, you stop and think for a moment. *I just fed him a half hour ago. How much did he take in at the last feeding? He seemed to feed well. What usually happens at this time of day?*

If you know where you are in your daily routine, you can answer those questions. You might realize, *Since he just ate, he's probably not hungry. Mmm, come to think of it, he's often cranky at this hour!* And you will consider other options to calm him, not just putting a bottle or your breast into his mouth.

Of course, it takes time to realize what your baby is trying to "say." But the first month of her life will give you lots of information. And if you're conscious of her routine, it will be easier for you to notice, for instance, that when she wakes up, she usually lets out a soft intermittent cry that tells you she's waiting for you to come to her and perhaps change her diaper. Or that when she's in her infant seat and lets out little noises, she's amusing herself. Or that when you hear a strong, urgent, uninterrupted cry, she's saying, "Come here. I need you *now!*"

With a fairly consistent routine, you are also more likely to accomplish your baby-care chores in a calm, orderly manner, which means that both you and your child will be relaxed. You will say to yourself, *I can do this. I am competent.* You won't feel tied down; you'll feel as if you're in charge. You will feel good about being a mother, which will only make you a better mother! The reverse is also true. If you're headed in the other direction, down that road of anxiety and self-doubt, it gets worse, not better. When a mother doesn't know what to do, she might panic, at which point she can't help another person, certainly not a baby. You have to remain calm and in control, and a routine will help you.

The routine gives you time just to relax with your baby. She's been here less than a month. When you handle the repetitive demands of your busy day with grace, you can also incorporate special times into your day just to be with your baby. The cuddling, the skin-to-skin contact, the loving glances, the gentle caresses, and the soft words and lullabies are the most important part of your routine, especially in these early weeks. They deepen your connection.

Creating a Good Routine

A good routine has four parts: nutrition (eating), playtime, physical and emotional care (such as bathing and massage), and sleep. Together, they are like the "classes" your baby attends at "newborn school." They occur and reoccur throughout the day. When your little one is well taught and cared for in each class, he's going to be a happy baby.

Nutrition. We must pay attention to how and when your baby eats. Eating at regular, well-spaced intervals helps him sleep better, play better, and have better digestion. He will grow and gain weight. At first, your baby will eat seven to eight times in a twenty-four-hour period. Ideally, we want to diminish the number during the night, so we must compensate by offering more feedings during the day.

Play. We make babies feel secure through hands-on connection, which is why play is such a vital part of the daily routine. You might not think of the time you spend holding, rocking, caressing, bathing, massaging, and even diapering your baby as play, but all of these interactions communicate love to him. Just as important, play puts a "space" after each feeding, so that he doesn't associate eating with sleep. Play stimulates your baby's body and brain. It helps him grow intellectually and physically and provides new opportunities for bonding, not just with you but also with others in the household. Newborns stay awake only for about a half hour at a stretch, and gradually, starting around the third week, they become more interested in and interactive with their surroundings. The most important play period for young babies involves bathing and massage, which I cover in chapter 11. In the evening, the bath/massage combination, followed by a "top-off" feeding, helps to prepare baby for the next "class," where he learns to sleep.

Sleep. Sleep—and the ability to fall asleep on your own—is essential for babies and grown-ups. Playtime at this age is at most thirty minutes. Otherwise, she'll get overtired. Before she cries, gently nudge her into the sleep "class." Help her get ready for sleep by making her room peaceful and dark. Slow down; swaddle her. Put her down in her crib awake, so she learns how to *self*-soothe, which is one of the most important lessons of sleep class.

◆ ◆ ◆

To sum up, the routine we're moving toward won't happen right away. Some days, in fact, it will seem as if there's no routine at all. But if you keep reinforcing the eat-play-sleep pattern, your baby's

---

TUMMY TIME

It's not too early to put your baby on her tummy for a few minutes. She might not like it at first, but if you lie on your stomach in front of her and talk to her, she will gradually get used to the position. Tummy time is especially important nowadays, because babies primarily sleep on their backs, so they need other opportunities to build back and neck muscles.

day will eventually look something like this: You'll feed him four times during the day—say at seven A.M., ten A.M., one P.M., and four P.M.—in short, every three hours. But at the end of the afternoon, you'll "cluster" his last two feedings, giving him "dinner" at six P.M., before his bath and massage. You'll put him into pajamas or a sleep sack, give him one extra feeding at seven thirty, swaddle him, and put him into bed.

In this first month, as you move from feeding to play and, once a day, bath and massage, your baby won't have much actual playtime after each feeding. At this age, he can easily get overstimulated, so keep face time—eye contact and goo-gooing—brief, let's say no more than thirty minutes. Don't wait until he's cranky. Help him wind down by rocking and rubbing his back. Then swaddle him and place him in his bassinet or crib when he is awake.

Your baby might take to this routine immediately. Or it will be a matter of trial and error as you get to know her. Try to be consistent: stick to the eat-play-sleep pattern.

Even when you follow the steps in each "class" perfectly, your baby will still cry at times—all babies cry. But she will learn the most important lesson: to self-soothe. Eventually, she will be able to amuse herself and fall asleep on her own. It won't happen by the end of this first month, but she will have the best possible start, thanks to your routine.

Be patient! This routine probably sounds like a lot of work, and it may feel strange to try something new. What happened with little Luigi happens with almost all babies. Some days your routine will be more consistent than others. It depends on you, your baby, and everything else in the household. Especially in the first month, you might spend the whole day dealing with a tired, cranky baby who seems to be in pain. You will spend time holding her, trying to comfort her, and the last thing you want to think about is her routine.

But please keep in mind that you are *teaching* her. You have to try again the next day—and the next. Some babies are harder to teach than others, just like children and adults. In order to have a calm, happy child, you need a plan, and you need to help your baby stick to it. A good routine is work, and it's worth it. It doesn't just benefit your child; it's also good for you. With a little time, you will have a baby who sleeps through the night. You will be able to sit down, talk with your husband, speak on the telephone with friends, and even take a bubble bath. It won't happen quickly. But after one tiring day, you'll finally be able to have dinner without anyone having to hold the baby, because she'll already be asleep.

How to Start Following a Routine

If you're breast-feeding, in the first days after your milk came in, your baby ate whenever he felt hungry, so feedings were every two hours or so. If infants are fed correctly and getting proper nutrition, most begin on their own to last longer from one feeding to the next. Once you see that your baby starts extending the time between feedings—for some, it happens as early as the second week—that's the point where you have to make sure he stays on that track and that the time between feedings keeps getting longer.

Initially, with formula-fed babies, there are fewer problems and less guesswork. We don't have to worry about proper latch-on or whether the mother is producing enough milk. You can see how much your baby takes in. Also, the amount of milk the baby can ingest is consistent at every feeding. (A breast-fed baby gets less at the end of the day, when Mom's milk production tends to diminish.) However, once Mom and baby get the hang of breast-feeding, these differences even out.

During this phase, when babies eat more frequently and stay awake for only half an hour after each feeding, try to have at least a few minutes of playtime. On some days, your baby might go back to sleep right after you feed him. This is fine; he will be awake after the next feeding. Just stay with it. Keep him awake during feedings and try to "insert" playtime after each meal. In the weeks ahead, he will stay awake for even longer stretches.

Routines naturally vary from baby to baby. It often takes more time to get a baby on a good routine because of low birth weight, eating difficulties, physical pain, or other hidden problems that cause discomfort, such as allergies. Temperament also plays into the equation. Some infants are harder to guide because they are sensitive, fussier by nature, or extremely active. They are not the majority. If you stick to a routine, even with a difficult-to-calm child, you will at least know what to do. In the sections ahead, I will help you stay on track for each part of your routine, so that you can avoid common mistakes. Remember, starting good habits is not easy, but it's a lot easier than having to change bad ones.

Chapter 10

EAT: GOOD FEEDING, GOOD ROUTINE

Eating starts a baby's day. I've seen formula-fed babies who take to the bottle immediately. And while breast-feeding can be initially trickier, I've also seen breast-fed babies who quickly learn how to latch on properly and suck efficiently. These "good eaters" eat at fairly regular intervals and burp easily after being fed. At the two-week checkup, they're almost back to their birth weight or have even surpassed it. They stay up for a half hour. And when they're swaddled and put to bed, most of the time they drift off to sleep with minimal crying. However, not all infants have such a trouble-free start. Feeding problems can happen to babies whether they're on breast milk or formula. Whereas it's relatively easy to nudge good eaters onto a good routine, infants who have initial feeding problems take longer to get there.

Our goal now is to get your baby to eat more efficiently and to work toward a predictable pattern of feedings. Instead of eating every two hours, as this month progresses, she'll nurse or take a bottle every three hours, going from as many as twelve meals a day to six or seven. Establishing a good feeding pattern can re-quire a lot of patience on your part—figuring out what your baby needs, calming her and trying to ease whatever is making her cry, and gauging how much milk your body produces. This chapter helps you answer three key questions:

> How efficiently and how often does your baby eat?

> What happens after your baby eats?

> What's happening to you?

Feeding problems escalate quickly. Although only a week or ten days has passed since your baby came home, that's his entire lifetime. By the end of this month, he'll be three times as old. *Now* is the time to troubleshoot!

How Efficiently and How Often Does Your Baby Eat?

When I'm on a job, it's sometimes easy for me to pinpoint a reason for a baby's eating problems. For example, he was premature and has a weak sucking reflex. More often, though, it's a combination of factors, each of which contributes to the problem. We've al-ready described some feeding challenges: sucking and latch-on problems, keeping your baby awake through feedings. Getting past these hurdles in the first few days at home is essential to giv-ing your newborn a good start. Otherwise, the following things might be happening:

Your baby isn't getting enough nutrition from his feedings. This is primarily a breast-feeding issue—often, an improper latch—but it can also happen to formula-fed babies who don't like to

BREAST-FEEDING DANGER SIGNS

Your baby might not be getting proper nutrition if...

• His mouth covers only the tip of the nipple, instead of at least part of the areola.
• You can't hear swallowing sounds.
• He gets frustrated and cries.
• He chews on your nipple instead of sucking.
• He falls asleep on the job.
• His urine is dark and sparse; his diaper is barely wet.

suck. Either way, if a baby doesn't get enough to eat, it can affect her disposition (she'll cry a lot), put her at risk for dehydration, and possibly thwart her physical development. If you suspect that your baby isn't ingesting enough, review chapters 6 and 7 on feeding basics and breast-feeding.

Pay particular attention to whether your baby is swallowing while nursing and to *how* your baby suckles. If he sucks without swallowing and you've nursed him for forty minutes or more, he might be staying on your breast for comfort, not food. It is not wise to allow this behavior, because it can traumatize your nipples. He might need extra sucking time—some babies do—but it should not be on your breast. I often suggest introducing a pacifier at ten days or older, but only if a baby has no problem latching on or sucking. If you're still having breast-feeding issues, let your baby suck on your pinkie finger for few minutes. Pull it out of his mouth when he starts to suck more slowly.

If by his two-week checkup, your baby is not at least on the way to regaining the 10 percent of birth weight that he lost, there may be an underlying health issue, but that's rarely the case. More often, a weight problem at this point is the result of a feeding issue.

Your baby's feedings take ten minutes or less. Infants' tummies are tiny. They need to eat often at first. But around the second week, most healthy babies are alert, stronger, and capable of more efficient suction. Your baby should start taking in more food in less time and go for a longer stretch between feedings. For example, if the morning feeding happened around seven A.M., then the next feeding should be three hours later, counting from the moment when the baby started nursing.

In a good feeding, the baby latches on, sucks a few times before she swallows, and then continues to nurse for around twenty minutes or so. Of course, there are variations, especially with breast-feeding. Some babies can satisfy themselves in a shorter time. Less efficient feeders might need up to forty minutes for a full feeding. However, if by two weeks old your baby seems to be slowing down or stops sucking altogether in the middle of a feeding, he might be on his way to becoming a "snacker." Because he doesn't consume enough and instead drifts off to sleep, he's hungry when he wakes. He'll eat too often and throughout the night. If you see this pattern developing, do something right away. Feed your baby with him wearing less clothing or only a diaper. Don't swing or rock him while he eats. And follow my earlier suggestions in chapter 6 for keeping your little sleepyhead awake.

Your baby fusses during feedings. This usually means he needs to be burped more frequently and then allowed to continue nursing until satisfied. Burping will help prevent him from regurgitating part of the ingested milk. Crying in the middle of a feeding can also be a sign that your little one is frustrated because he's not getting enough milk. So if your baby is not sucking properly or is having latch-on problems after the first week and you can't correct it on your own by reading this chapter, it's probably time to get a lactation consultant to help you.

WHAT IF . . . My Baby Suddenly "Forgets" How to Breast-Feed?

If your baby seems to have gotten off to a good start with breast-feeding and then suddenly rejects your nipple, perhaps you introduced a bottle or a pacifier too early, before he mastered the art of sucking. Many professionals call this nipple confusion. But it can also happen even before a pacifier is given. Some babies simply "forget" how to suck on the nipple. They're different situations, but both are stressful for mother and child.

If your baby balks at breast-feeding after being fed with a bottle or given a pacifier, it's not really confusion, it's preference. Sucking on a pacifier or bottle nipple requires a different kind of sucking than on the breast. So if you offer your baby a silicone nipple before he has mastered the art of sucking a human one, it can interfere with the learning process.

On the other hand, if your baby seems suddenly to forget how to nurse, it's often a matter of frustration. Maybe your milk is coming down too slowly. She can't start to suck until the milk starts to flow. And when she can't suck, she cries. That only makes it worse. The crying keeps her mouth open, and the more you try to nurse her, the more she'll squirm and cry. She won't want to continue sucking.

Regardless of the reason, when your baby rejects your breast, instead of latching on properly when you start to feed, she will cry and keep searching for your nipple. But the more you try to get her to nurse, the more she cries. Don't give up. You might require professional help, but first try what works for me:

• Calm your baby when unsuccessful attempts to latch on upset her.

• Place your pinkie in her mouth, palm up (fingernail on the bottom), and let her suck for a few seconds. While she sucks on your finger, she is at least practicing sucking, and the pinkie tip is not much different from a human nipple.

- When she is calm, bring her to your breast again.

- If your baby refuses to suck, use a spoon or eyedropper to place a drop of breast milk on your nipple while she is trying to suck. Those few drops of liquid will activate her swallowing reflex. She will instinctively close her mouth over your nipple and begin to nurse. (If breast milk is not available and your baby is not on any formula supplement, use a few drops of bottled water or any safe drinking water.)

What Happens After Your Baby Eats?

Ideally, your baby "plays" after he eats. He's less than a full month old, so at this stage, spending time with him after a feeding is more of an opportunity to bond than to actually play. Still, we start now to create a "space" between eating and sleeping that later becomes a play period. That's the ideal. Here are some other possibilities.

Your baby is crying after a feeding. Perhaps you think she's hungry. As I pointed out earlier, new moms often misread crying as hunger. Let's say your baby has a good feeding at seven A.M., nursing for at least twenty minutes. She stays up for a little while, and then you swaddle her and put her down. If she starts crying at eight fifteen, don't immediately assume that she's hungry. It's been less than two hours since her last meal. Before feeding her again, try to comfort her. Burp her again, and hold her in an upright position. Patting her back gently might help her expel any air that's trapped in her tummy. Swaddle her again, and continue to hold her over your shoulder in an upright position. Then place her back in her crib.

She might go to sleep. Or she might begin to turn her face from side to side, searching for something to suck again. If you've already introduced a pacifier, give it to her. If not, let her suck on your pinkie for a few minutes for comfort. But please, if you do decide to feed her, even though it has been less than two hours since her last feeding, give her a proper feeding. Don't feed her for a few minutes and try to put her down again. Otherwise, you'll reinforce her tendency to snack instead of having a full meal.

Let me explain. Crying burns calories and, therefore, makes a baby hungry. So when your baby is up and fussing after a feeding or a too-short nap, she will be hungry much sooner than if she had gone to sleep. And then, when you start to feed her, guess what? She will be so tired that she falls asleep on the job and wakes up hungry a short time after. Try to avoid this by sticking to regular bedtimes and paying attention to how long she can stay up without becoming cranky. Throughout the day, put her into her crib before she gets overtired.

Your baby seems to be in pain. Some babies feel uncomfortable after a feeding, so they cry. Most often, the problem is gas, although it could also be a more serious digestive issue, such as reflux or colic. Even the happiest baby has some discomfort from gas. His source of nutrition is milk, which builds a huge amount of bubbles in his tummy. A gassy baby pulls his legs up to his chest and cries. His little face gets red. His fists are clenched, and his whole body is tense.

To help dispel air swallowed during the feeding, keep him upright—his body is in a straight line. Rub his back in an upward motion to try to get him to burp. You might be tempted to burp him in one of the other burp positions (chapter 6), but laying him down or across your lap or even having him sit on your lap might increase his pain. A walk around the house can help, too, especially with up-and-down movements. I find that walking up and down two steps can help.

Your baby spits up. When your baby burps and expels air, a little amount of milk comes out through her mouth and/or nose. There's no reason for concern; babies often spit up. However, if your baby was born before term—that is, three weeks or more before your due date—the valve in her stomach was not fully developed. Normally, that valve prevents food from coming up. But if it's not working, your baby might regurgitate large amounts while you're feeding her or when you lay her down. She's also likely to cry. The problem could be reflux—baby heartburn, which is common in small and premature babies—or another kind of gastric issue. Talk to your pediatrician. (See more in chapter 15 on gas, reflux, and colic, which tend to get worse during the second month.)

Your baby is overtired. We tend to keep newborns awake for longer than we should. Babies need rest. After burping and a diaper change, a properly fed baby in the first month can stay up for anywhere from a few to thirty minutes. If your baby is staying up longer at this age, especially if she gets passed around like a little football to visitors, she can get overtired. Her immature nervous system cannot handle so much stimulation. She complains by crying. Even worse, the crying will make her hungry. Instead of risking the "snacking" pattern I describe above, be especially careful now about keeping your baby's life very simple. Feed her in a calm, dimly lit place. Hold her upright for at least fifteen minutes after a meal. Get her into her crib before she starts crying.

Your baby goes longer than three hours between feedings. With a month-old baby, this pattern tells me that despite my advice to the contrary, you believe in that old rule about never waking a sleeping baby. If you're breast-feeding, it also tells me that you might not be paying attention to your own body. I can still remember my mother doing housework and suddenly standing still. She'd touch her breast and say, "The baby is hungry!" When you feel your breasts fill, it's usually time for a feeding.

Remember that babies are on a twenty-four-hour clock when they're born. At this stage, we need to get them used to spending more time awake during the day. If your baby doesn't wake up on his own for his daytime feedings, lift him gently out of bed and put him over your shoulder. If he doesn't wake immediately, change his diaper. Talk to him softly. "Wake up, little sleepyhead!" Undressed, feeling the air on his skin, and lying on his back will usually rouse him. You'll know he is still hungry whether he cries or not, because he'll root and move around as if searching for food.

Most babies will continue to be hungry at night at one month old, but as they begin to take in more, they can go for longer intervals without eating. But if daytime feedings are too far apart—say, longer than three or three and a half hours—your baby will need to catch up on her feedings at night. And it will take you much longer to establish a good routine.

What's Happening to You?

If all has gone well, feeding during the first month is relatively tension-free. But if your baby is having a hard time, you might wonder whether you're breast-feeding properly, whether the Chinese food you had for dinner is causing your baby pain, whether something is wrong with your milk, or whether you're producing "enough." As I pointed out earlier, the stress alone can reduce a nursing mother's milk supply. So if you didn't follow my earlier advice about caring for yourself, start now. Resting, eating well, and drinking more water than you normally do will most likely stimulate your milk production.

How will you know if your body is not producing enough

milk? If your baby hasn't regained the birth weight she lost by her two-week checkup, it might mean that she is having trouble extracting breast milk or that your body isn't producing enough. Most often, it's a combination of the two, a vicious cycle. Sucking stimulates the release of milk, but if there's not enough milk, a baby can become too weak to suck.

For example, Oliver, a baby I took care of from the day he came home, was losing weight even though he was feeding regularly. We kept him on a very tight feeding schedule, making sure that he ate every three hours, at least. Oliver had a strong sucking reflex, but Helen, his mother, was producing too little milk. Oliver had to work very hard to get it, and the sucking used up whatever "fuel" he got from eating.

Over the years, I've found that the best way to increase a mother's milk production is to do a combination of breast-feeding and then, so as not to exhaust the baby, giving expressed breast milk in a bottle. Helen allowed Oliver ten minutes on each breast. She then pumped both breasts (at the same time) for another ten minutes. An electric pump is best for this; a manual pump would have taken too long. The idea is to send a message to the mother's body to increase her milk production. Oliver didn't have to work as hard to get his mother's milk from a bottle, because liquids flow more easily through a silicone nipple. After a week of being very conscientious and aggressive about feeding, Helen's milk supply increased, Oliver started to gain weight normally, and we all could relax.

In Helen's case, she simply wasn't producing enough breast milk. Other mothers have milk-supply issues because their breasts produce less as the day goes on. Their babies tend to cry more at the end of the day, or they wake frequently at night. The afternoon and early-evening feeds aren't enough to sustain them. For this, pumping is an effective solution. Wait for ten minutes after the morning feeding—a time when your body produces the most milk—and pump both breasts. That way, your body gets the message that more milk is needed. When feeding your baby later in the day, you can nurse your baby and supplement that with the expressed milk you pumped earlier.

If you didn't follow my advice about breast care and your nipples are now cracked and/or sore, you might unconsciously be holding yourself away from your baby, making it hard for him to latch on. If you've been suffering for more than a day or two, though, call your doctor.

It also might help to switch breast-feeding positions. Experiment to see what feels and works best for the two of you. With small babies—often the ones who have trouble latching on—I first recommend the cross hold. If that doesn't work, I suggest the football hold, which gives you good control of your baby's head as he roots around, trying to latch on.

Chapter 11

PLAY: BATHING AND MASSAGE

I became a baby nurse because I care very deeply about giving children a good start in life. One of the best ways you can prepare your baby for the future and help her have a better life is to pay attention to the physical and emotional care you give day after day: how you diaper, dress, hold, and caress her and, most important, how you massage and bathe her.

Touch is a big part of childcare. The first feelings of love for another person come through skin-to-skin contact—and not just in humans. Animals use touch with their beaks, noses, or paws. I remember being a child in rural Brazil. On lazy, hot days, the domestic animals that dotted the countryside would take a break from the heat. The little ones would come to their mothers' sides to be nudged and cuddled. Even the adult animals took advantage of skin touching. Touch is the way they show affection—it's part of their lives . . . and of ours.

Touching a baby is vitally important. It is, as I said earlier, the most critical element of the "play" part of the routine for a very young baby who sleeps most of the time. This first month is a time to introduce your baby to comforting rituals that involve touch—

bathing, massage, swaddling, and cuddling. She will gradually get used to the new sensations of being submerged in water and being caressed. By the end of the second or third month, when you no longer have to swaddle her, your baby's evening playtime will consist of bath, massage, and pajamas.

Playing with your baby at this age means connecting with her. Whether you lie on a bed or on the floor with her, talk to her. While she's in her carriage, or when you're sitting comfortably in a chair, talk to her. All of these moments with your baby involve cuddling, caressing, and closeness.

The Bath

A warm bath, lovingly given by Mom, tells the baby that play is over; we're winding down. It calms and cleans him. Although you can only give your baby a sponge bath at first, at some point during the second or third week, after the umbilical cord has fallen off, he can handle a "real" bath. Once you are able to bathe your baby, do it daily, because it's a pleasant, relaxing end-of-the-day ritual that helps your baby know when bedtime is approaching.

Make sure you are totally available and free of interruptions before you start, which should be about an hour before bedtime. Feed your baby first; a baby with a full tummy will enjoy his bath more than a hungry baby.

Preparing the Bath

Get everything you need ahead of time: a small cloth or a sponge to wash the baby's body, cotton balls or squares, "tearless" baby shampoo, a plastic pitcher or container with warm water, and two towels, one for drying and one to use as a cover during the massage. You'll also want to have within easy reach a diaper, a comb, and a soft brush to wash his head, a nonscented oil for massaging him afterward, and a clean pair of pajamas.

I prefer using a portable tub for a baby this age. You can also use a large sink if you have at least a foot of clearance between the faucets and the basin. Make sure that the bathing area is not under a vent that dispenses cold air. Ideally, the room temperature is between seventy-five and seventy-nine degrees Fahrenheit. Using your elbow to feel the water temperature will give you the best idea of what the water will feel like to your baby. It should feel comfortable on your skin, warm but not hot.

Getting Baby Used to the Water

When you first bathe your baby, he might start to cry as soon as his clothes are removed and he is placed in the water. That's because he feels unprotected. To make him feel more comfortable, put a cloth diaper on his chest as soon as you undress him, even before you place him in the bath. Hold him over the tub, and lower him into the water slowly, back first. Avoid making sudden movements, which will scare him. Initially, he might tense up, suggesting that he feels insecure. Talk to him, and hold him firmly.

For the first few baths, keep a wet diaper or washcloth on the baby's chest. It will help him get used to the water and start to relax. Some babies get accustomed right away; others take longer. Little by little, your baby will begin to enjoy the experience. When you sense that he feels more comfortable in the water, it's no longer necessary to cover him.

Washing Body and Hair

Clean your baby's eyes with a moist washcloth. Start in the corner of the eye, and move toward the ear. Wash her body with a sponge or a washcloth. Gently wash the pleat on her neck and under her arms. Using the little pitcher, pour warm water on the remaining portions of her body to keep her warm. Once a baby is old enough to be immersed in water, I like to shampoo her head every day.

After the Tub

When I lift the baby from the tub, I wrap her in the first towel to get most of the water off her. Then I remove the wet towel and wrap her in a soft, dry one and rub her body slowly to warm and dry her. I like hooded towels, because they keep the baby's wet head from getting a chill. While I'm drying her, I continue to do gentle touching all over her body through the cotton towel. This feels comforting and is good preparation for massage.

If she is still calm, I then give her a massage (see below). However, if she is already tired and crying, I get her into her pajamas quickly. She is either cold or too tired for further stimulation—or both. Instead, I top her off with another feeding, swaddle her, and send her off to dreamland, which I talk about in chapter 12.

WHAT IF . . . **My Baby Sweats a Lot?**

Sometimes it's the weather, but also some babies sweat more than others. When a baby sweats a lot, I shampoo twice a day, in the morning under a sink faucet and at night in the tub.

Making the Most of Massage

Massage gives your baby his first awareness of his body. We know that in the first year, a baby doesn't quite have a sense of self. He's part of his environment, not separate from it, and he's not sure where he ends and Mommy begins. This is why you are so important in these early months. In his mind, he doesn't exist without you!

When you massage your baby, gently and lovingly—just for a few minutes at first and longer as she gets older—it not only calms her down, but it also helps her feel loved and cared for. Massage also allows you to tune into your baby. It gives you a sense of connecting to her. You can feel where her little body tenses, and you can tend to her with more "information." Massaging her body deepens your bond. You have to take it a lot more slowly with some infants at first, because they are either more physically frail or more sensitive to stimulation, but most eventually come to love it.

Babies in my care are always massaged daily. They become children who love to be touched and who know how to relax. For example, one day I asked one of "my" babies, who had by then grown into a talkative toddler with very definite opinions, "Do you want a massage or not?"

"*Yes!*" he exclaimed. This was a two-year-old who was as busy as can be. The only time he loved to be quiet and would lie still was during his daily massage. And although I was thinking, *Maybe I'll skip his massage tonight,* he wanted that massage! I can't say that it's only because of massage, but the babies in my care are not cranky. They are not perfect, either, but they are usually happy.

Another reason touch is so important is that society has changed. Most mothers have to work in addition to caring for their babies. If you're away from your baby all day, it's important to carve out special time to reconnect. Massage is a great use of your time.

How to Introduce Your Baby to Massage

Usually after the first week, even before a baby is able to take a bath, I start with a gentle massage. Proceed slowly, as you would with anything that is new to your baby. Some, usually the more sensitive infants, protest at first. But if massage is introduced gently, as days go by, most get used to the stimulation and start enjoying it.

During the first month, massage your baby on the changing table or wherever you change her diaper. Start with brief massages. During the first week especially, your baby is fragile. As with first baths, she might not like to be undressed, and she gets cold easily.

When you're first getting your baby accustomed to your touch, it's best to cover her with a towel or a cloth diaper. Why not touch your baby directly? Some babies are on the skinny side, fragile, and/or more sensitive than others. So it's best to be extra gentle at first. A baby massage is different from a vigorous adult massage, more about connecting than about stimulating.

Your baby might need to be massaged through a light cover for as long as the first three weeks. However, it's the touching that matters. That's why premature babies who are massaged gain weight faster.

Don't be in a hurry. Whether your baby takes to massage quickly or needs more time to get used to it, massage will help you connect with her physical being and help you see how she likes to be touched. Press down lightly, applying gentle pressure, just enough to feel her little body. Use delicate strokes. Also, watch your own breathing; it should be slow and steady.

At first, spend no more than five minutes. Start with the bottoms of her feet, gently kneading them. Make clockwise movements with both hands. Then move on to her arms, massaging her tiny palms with your thumb. Also massage clockwise on her tummy. Do her face last—around the mouth, between the eyebrows, around the ears. Then turn her onto her tummy, and massage her legs and back.

This is a great time to connect. While you're massaging your baby, you might want to talk to her, name her body's parts. However, every mom has her own style. It's OK to be silent and play soft music instead. Whatever you do, the most important thing is that you keep doing the same things, so that your baby comes to expect it.

Eventually, depending on your baby and when you start, you'll be able to massage your baby's skin directly. At that point, you will need something to lubricate her skin. I like oils better than lotions, because your hands travel more smoothly over an oiled baby's body.

Whatever you apply to your baby's skin will be absorbed into her body. Therefore, don't use commercial oils—they are petroleum-based and perfumed. (If you recall, I use petroleum jelly to prevent diaper rash. That's because it provides a barrier to moisture, but I wouldn't want to apply it all over a baby's body.) In my opinion, all-natural fruit oils are best, because we cook with them. If we can eat them, it's fine if they're also absorbed through our pores. I like avocado oil, which I've found to be safe on most babies' skin.

WHAT IF . . . My Baby Seems to React Badly to Massage?

If your baby's skin gets irritated or she develops a rash, if she coughs or sneezes or gets cranky during the massage, it's probably not the massage itself. More likely, it's what you're using on

her body. Even a so-called natural oil can be problematic, so base
your choice on your baby, not on you. You might love the scent
of a particular product, but you don't know how your baby's skin
will react until you actually try it. At one month, it's too early to
know whether your baby has any allergies—say, to nuts. But if
nut allergies run in the family, be extra careful. Read the label,
and look at the ingredients. If an oil, for example, is nut-free, try
it for a few days on a part of her body that's not near her face,
such as her lower leg. If she has any kind of bad reaction, try a
different product instead.

Once you begin to massage your baby's body directly, proceed
as you did when she was covered with the towel. However, wipe
any oil or lotion off your hands before you do her face. As weeks
go by, and your baby gets used to your touch, gradually increase
touch time. You can then massage her on a firm bed (no water-
beds) or the floor. If the latter, place a blanket or towels down to
provide a cushion between your baby and the floor. You should
be comfortable, too, able to sit down, cross or open your legs, and
lean forward to reach her.

Remember the importance of touch, and think about how
happy your baby will feel to be softly caressed by his mother. A
light, delicate touch with little to no pressure is all that is needed.
As he grows and becomes stronger, you can increase the pressure
a bit. Your hands must work delicately but at the same time be
firm, slow, and rhythmic. By taking it slowly, you will know what
makes your own baby happy. As you massage him, always keep
in mind that this is an act of love more than anything. Your baby
feels your love through your hands, and it will calm and center
him. In a sense, it is the beginning of his emotional education.

Chapter 12

SLEEP: SENDING BABY TO DREAMLAND

When I meet a client, the first question—even before the baby arrives—is "Can you help my baby sleep through the night?" I have found that of all parts of the routine, parents care most about sleep, especially mothers. Who can blame them? Everyone knows that newborns mean sleepless nights, sometimes for months on end.

At first, you probably didn't mind waking up a few times in the middle of the night to feed your little one. It's all new and exciting. But by the second or third week, as you become more and more sleep-deprived, you start to long for at least a few hours of sleep without interruptions.

How do we get an infant to sleep through the night? The quick answer is *gradually*.

Sleeping Through the Night

Let's look at what "sleeping through the night" means. Babies sleep in similar cycles to adults, going in and out of a deep sleep every forty-five minutes or so, but they aren't quite like adults. When we wake up, we turn to the other side and go back to sleep. But babies don't know how to put themselves back to sleep after each cycle. Our job is to help them learn how.

In my experience, it takes six to ten weeks for babies to sleep with only two wake-ups during the night. If they are getting enough to eat during the day and learn how to put themselves back to sleep at night, they finally "sleep through the night." In the best-case scenario, by two months a baby's bedtime is between six and eight, often the later time because Mom likes to wait for Dad to come home. The baby falls asleep on her own, with little or no help. She has an eleven P.M. feeding, a fast diaper change and burp—no chatting in between—and then back to bed. She will continue to wake for a three A.M. feeding, but as she gains weight and can last increasingly longer, that middle-of-the-night feeding will gradually become her morning meal.

It doesn't always happen that way or that easily. But if you keep in mind what you're moving toward and at least *try* to establish a consistent routine now, you will build up trust, which makes sleep training easier. Now, while your baby is still in the first month, is the time to teach her the right lessons in "sleep class."

The Keys to a Good Sleep Routine

On some days (and nights), your baby's sleep pattern will be erratic. He's still less than a month old, and it's unlikely that he can sleep for more than four hours, because his tummy is so small that hunger will wake him up. For a few days, he might sleep for a longer stretch and then start waking more frequently again. But if you really keep at it, consistently repeating the eat-play-sleep pattern during the day—ideally, every three hours—your baby will start sleeping more soundly. This phase won't last for long if you follow these suggestions. If you don't, you might still be dealing with sleep issues when your baby is a year old. Keep the following pointers in mind.

Discourage early wake-ups. We tend to rush to a baby as soon as she makes her first noise. Try not to. Sometimes it's hard to persuade an "early bird" not to start her day at five A.M., but you have to try. When your baby cries, wait a few minutes to see if she gets distracted and perhaps falls back to sleep. In this way, you are teaching your child the right sleep lesson: to entertain herself and stay in bed a little longer without your help. Decide what's a reasonable wake-up hour in your household: six A.M., seven A.M.? If she wakes up before that, you might have to feed her again, but after a good burp, put her right back to bed, as if it is the middle of the night.

Step in before he gets too tired. Figure out what "tired" looks like in your baby. It all depends on the child. Maybe yours fusses a little or gets cranky. End playtime immediately, and get him ready for sleep before he gets overtired and starts to cry. Some babies also conk out without warning while in a bouncy chair or car seat. With such a young baby, it's OK just to let him stay there. But as he gets older, it's better for him to sleep comfortably in his own bed.

Put your baby in her crib when she's awake. If your baby is generally easygoing and you start her bedtime ritual before she gets overtired, when you lay her down she might fuss a little but then fall asleep. Or not. As I've said repeatedly, some babies have a harder time settling down than others. You might have to pick her up again, burp her, and change her diaper if needed. If she's still uncomfortable, you'll hold her a bit more and then lay her down again.

Don't talk to your baby when you comfort him. Talking is a natural thing to do. We think that verbal reassurance helps calm a baby who fusses while trying to go to sleep or wakes up in the middle of the night. It actually has the opposite effect. I control

THE SEVEN SLEEP STEPS

Here are the steps to creating a sleep environment for your baby, a "classroom" that calms her and "teaches" her that it's time to sleep. Setting a particular bedtime is up to you, but keep it on the early side. The whole process takes about an hour. I begin at around five P.M. during the winter and six P.M. during the summer when it stays lighter out. I'm also flexible, give or take thirty minutes, in case a grandparent or other visitor comes around.

1. Take your baby away from the hubbub of the household.
2. Give her a bath, followed by a massage. Put on her night clothes.
3. Pull the shades to darken her room.
4. Feed, burp, and check her diaper. By now, an hour or so has passed.
5. Swaddle the baby.
6. Hold her upright for ten minutes if she has no digestive issues, twenty minutes if she spits up after meals or tends to cry when laid down.
7. Put her into the crib while she's awake. Turn on music or a white-noise machine, because sound is a good distraction while she's settling down.

That's the ideal. When a baby is calm, looking around, I give her a chance to fall asleep on her own. Your baby might have to be held longer and then put down. She might be calm when you're holding her, but when you put her into her crib, she begins to fuss. Don't rush in to "rescue" her. She might just be settling herself. If she begins to cry, first try to calm her in the crib. If that doesn't work, you might have to give her a pacifier or pick her up and reposition her. You might have to hold her until she calms down. The important thing is to try to stay calm yourself. Do this as many times as necessary. Remember that you're *teaching* her.

my urge to talk, reminding myself that the warmth of my body and the act of comforting itself—holding, rocking back and forth—is enough to reassure the baby that he is not alone and is being well cared for. Also, as your baby gets older, if you chat and smile, he will think of naptime or nighttime as playtime, and he will awaken even more often.

Set reasonable bedtimes. Remember what I said earlier about paying a "price" for keeping your baby awake when he's tired or keeping him up at night. If Daddy wants extra time with his baby, he should change his work schedule instead of depriving his son or daughter of sleep.

The Pacifier: A Good Sleep Aid

All babies need to be calmed before sleeping. Bathing and massaging, darkening the room, and cuddling all teach your child what to expect at bedtime. The more you repeat these sleep rituals, the sooner your baby will associate them with sleep. But he also might need extra help.

The pacifier is one of my favorite good sleep aids, because it gives your baby a chance to suck without being on your breast. When infants are hungry, stimulated, or upset, they instinctively search for something to suck. In some babies, the need to suck diminishes during the first month; in others, it continues. In either situation, a pacifier helps. It makes the job of soothing a baby easier. And it's the safest and healthiest alternative to *you* becoming a sleep aid yourself, a problem I describe below.

Admittedly, pacifiers also require your participation. If your baby wakes in the middle of the night and needs her pacifier to fall back to sleep, you have to get out of bed and give it to her, until she's old enough to find it herself, usually around five or six months. Still, pacifiers are indispensable when it comes to calming a baby.

I typically introduce a pacifier in the second week, once breast-feeding is going well. Formula-fed babies, on the other hand, are already used to sucking on a silicone nipple, so it's fine to use a pacifier earlier if your baby needs extra soothing.

The first time you offer your baby a pacifier, it might seem as if she's trying to spit it out. It's not because she doesn't like it. It's because she doesn't know how to suck on it. Newborns tend to push out when they suck. Hold the pacifier in her mouth to help her suck on it. Just be patient, and try a few times. She'll get it.

I limit my use of pacifiers. I don't automatically pop a pacifier into a baby's mouth when I put her down to sleep, unless she is crying. But when I have a fussy or hard-crying baby, I am happy to offer a pacifier. The sucking enables her to deal with whatever uncomfortable feelings she experiences as she drifts off to sleep. I might also give her a pacifier to distract her in an automobile on a long trip. Using a pacifier also prevents unnecessary feedings and helps a baby enjoy the time she spends in her crib, before and after sleeping.

I know that many parents do not like their children using a pacifier because they find it offensive. Some say they don't want their child walking around with a pacifier in public places. I agree, which is why the babies in my care don't even use their pacifiers around the house. Except for a long car trip or airplane ride, the pacifier stays in the crib. Other parents are against pacifiers because they fear that using one will harm their children's teeth. But I've never seen proof of this.

Remember that your baby won't use a pacifier forever. You will gradually progress to the point where you offer the pacifier only when necessary. The cutoff point varies from baby to baby. It depends on how often the pacifier is given and how much sucking and soothing the baby needs. If you notice that your baby is not particularly interested in his pacifier, it means he's not very dependent on it. It should be a simple matter to wean him off it. But even if he loves his pacifier, little by little, he will learn to distract himself in other ways, which will eventually diminish his need to suck on it. He also might discover his fingers and prefer to suck them instead.

Other Good Sleep Aids

I don't believe in having a lot of items in your baby's crib, both for safety reasons and because we don't want to overstimulate your baby. But a few well-chosen sleep aids, either fastened to the crib rails or placed on the mattress within your baby's line of sight, can help calm and distract her. She will learn to look for them and gradually become attached to them. In time, she will reach for them on her own. They soothe her with touch and sound and also amuse her visually.

Touch: comfort items. A month-old infant is too young to "adopt" a security item, something that he holds on to that he finds soothing, such as a small, soft blanket or a cuddly stuffed animal. But we can introduce the idea now and get your baby used to having the object nearby. Just place it in the crib next to him. In time, he will associate it with sleep and look for it whenever he wakes up and needs comforting.

Sounds: music. I recommend placing a CD player or iPod or another type of soothing "sound machine" in the nursery. You can play classical music or nature sounds or broadcast white noise that masks unwanted and possibly disturbing sounds from your household. One of my favorites is the Fisher-Price musical aquarium that hangs on the side of the crib. The colorful fishes swimming, the bubbles bouncing, and the soft lights glowing soothe most babies to sleep.

Visual distraction. When your baby is awake, it's important to give him time to discover his environment without your help. So it makes sense to provide things for him to look at in his crib. In the early 1960s, a scientist who tested the vision and hearing of babies in the delivery room verified that newborns can hear and see from the moment of birth. Other researchers showed that although babies are most attracted to human faces, they also are drawn to pictures that have great contrast between light and dark and strong colors, such as black and red.

These discoveries inspired me many years ago to make my own drawings and place them in the crib. Now shiny cardboard pictures are available in most baby stores. Mom can use anything that has shapes and color. It also can be a book, propped up and opened to a colorful page. Place them first on one side of the crib and then on the other to encourage your baby to turn his head and look in both directions.

These colorful images, along with a mobile hanging over the crib, are good sleep associations, because they help distract your baby when he's trying to fall asleep. They also amuse him when he wakes up and encourage him to stay in his crib longer, something all moms appreciate.

Teaching the Wrong Lessons in "Sleep Class"

You can't know in advance what kind of baby you're going to have or whether he's ever going to be a "good sleeper." But you can at least try to go with the flow. A pacifier and other good sleep associations will help your baby develop self-soothing skills. But even with these aids, it will take time for your baby to learn the lessons of "sleep class." If you get impatient and grab at solutions that work in the moment, sleep class doesn't go as planned. Let me explain how this happens.

We are creatures of habit, especially when it comes to sleep. Perhaps you have a friend who can only sleep with a small pillow between her knees. She even travels with it. If she wakes in the middle of the night, she probably rolls from one side to the other, instinctively grabbing for her pillow, because she needs it to get comfortable again. If the pillow has fallen onto the floor, she can't get back to sleep without it.

The same thing happens to a baby. Once he becomes attached to an object that helps him sleep, he won't be able to settle down when it's not there. In infancy, sleep associations initially come from the mother, his first sleep teacher. If she nurses or feeds him and allows him to fall asleep while on her breast, or if she walks or swings him to help him fall asleep, when he wakes in the middle of the night, he doesn't know how to put himself back to sleep. He needs his mother. Like your friend's pillow, Mom has become the "object" that he associates with sleep. He'll need it—her—each time he awakens.

He might mutter or fuss a bit at first. If Mom doesn't appear, those little sounds become bigger and turn into crying. Eventually, his sleepy mom has to go into his room and do what she's always done to lull him back to sleep: feed him, carry him, rock him. That pattern can reoccur from one to ten times during the night.

If that scene sounds familiar, it means that your baby is learning that to fall asleep he needs you. And there's a good chance that for the next many months, you'll be out of bed several times in the middle of the night.

Any adult in your household can create a "bad" sleep association. In one family, before I was hired, the father had gotten into the habit of taking a drive with his baby girl to get her to fall asleep. Now she could only fall asleep in a car. One day, the father was busy and asked the baby-sitter to do the honors. The baby-sitter used the opportunity to take the father's brand-new SUV for a spin on a nearby freeway. She returned home with a sleeping baby *and* a speeding ticket.

The moral of this story is that everything you do teaches your baby what to expect. Sometimes, for instance, a mother who has to deal constantly with her baby's gas pains will ask if it's OK to take the baby into the living room. I can understand why. Everyone is there watching television. If she has company, Mom doesn't feel so alone. She can pass the baby around and give others a chance to soothe him. As tempting as it is, though, it's best not to consider this—unless you think it's a good idea for your baby to become accustomed to flitting from lap to lap. Remember, everything you do teaches your baby.

Most parents love to hold their infants to sleep. They don't weigh much, and they easily fall asleep while held. But when a baby starts to demand more attention and to protest when his mom or dad tries to lay him down, his parents get confused and upset. They want to change his behavior so that he falls asleep in his own bed. But the child has already learned the behavior, and his parents will have to work hard to reverse the pattern.

Always ask yourself, *What am I teaching my baby?* That in order to go to sleep, a grown-up must hold him? That Mommy is his "pacifier"? That there's no specific time for bed? Or that he goes to bed when the adults do? When you develop practices that make you or another adult your baby's only source of comfort, you are using "bad" sleep associations.

These practices might work, and at first, they might even make you happy. When your infant sucks on your breast, it releases chemicals in your brain that cause you to relax and feel content. Bad sleep associations also won't feel like a "problem" in the beginning, because once you get your newborn to sleep, it's easy to transfer her to her bassinet or crib without waking her. But when she is two or three months old, the minute you try to separate her from the warmth of your body, she'll wake up.

In my opinion, the most important advice I can give you is to teach your baby how to sleep without being rocked or nursed, without having to be swung or driven, without having to engage the whole household. There will be times when it's a good idea to nurse a baby to sleep. For example, after a baby is circumcised, I put him on Mom's breast to calm him. But he is (at most) eight days old at that point, and, as I warn the mother, this is a special circumstance, not an everyday practice.

Remember, too, that reinforcing bad sleep associations will also make it difficult for others to care for and calm your baby. I've heard a baby cry and cry until Mom (and only Mom) returns and "rescues" her. In my opinion, rocking and nursing your baby to sleep should be used sparingly and carefully. It might feel wonderful now, but think ahead to a few months from now. Will you feel OK when she needs you in order to fall asleep? If you've already started down this road, now is the easiest time to change bad habits.

SLEEP WARNINGS

+ *Don't put your baby to sleep directly after a feeding.* I must repeat again, your baby needs to get used to having a space—play—between eating and sleep, even if it's just ten minutes at first. At this age, playtime means holding and cooing at him during the day, bath and massage before bedtime.
+ *Don't use his bed as a play area.* Let him play elsewhere—say, in a little seat where you can talk to him or on the floor under a Gymini where he can amuse himself. Only when it's time for sleep should you place him in his bed.
+ *Don't teach him to depend solely on you for soothing.* In this first month, we can pretty safely assume that if an otherwise healthy baby can't settle down to sleep or cries, something is making him upset. Of course, you will soothe him. But it's also important to help him learn how to comfort himself. Any practice that requires you to be there all the time will set up a bad pattern that later needs to be changed.

When the Going Gets Tough, Keep Going

Any baby, even an "angel," will have moments of discomfort that interrupt his sleep. Gabriel, for example, weighed seven pounds at birth and at two weeks old had already regained his lost birth weight. Barely three weeks old, he was having a last feeding at around seven P.M., waking up at around two A.M., and sleeping uninterrupted for up to six hours. Admittedly, this is rare. Most babies at this age sleep for approximately a four-hour stretch during the night.

It didn't last. Gabe started having gas pains. Every night, around seven when he went to bed, he'd pull his legs up tight to his chest. He'd wake up again shortly after falling asleep. His mom, Samantha, who'd considered herself "lucky" until now, was very anxious. Was it really just gas? How could she help Gabe through the painful spasms?

At my suggestion, Samantha spent extra time burping Gabe before laying him down. Because we weren't sure which position Gabe preferred, sometimes she hoisted him over her shoulder, next to her chest in a vertical position. Other times, she tried laying him across her knees, facedown. Gabe stopped crying faster when his body was upright, so she continued that way. As soon as he was calm, Samantha placed him in his crib. She also gave him a pacifier, because he was eating well at that point.

For most babies, gas pains peak between four and six weeks and then start to calm down. In Gabe's case, they went on for almost a month, sometimes waking him at night. There was no miracle "cure." On his worst days, Samantha resigned herself to going in and out of his room several times. I kept telling her, "This is just for now. He'll grow out of it," and that helped her.

As it turned out, on most nights, Gabe required very little calming. And on some nights, he needed more. Gabe took to the pacifier easily, which is not always the case. And unlike some babies, whose gas pains increase as they take in larger amounts of milk, Gabe's didn't get worse.

I urged Samantha to take care of herself, too, which made *her* calmer on the days that Gabe was gassy. By the time Gabe weighed thirteen pounds, the gas diminished, and he could again last for a six- or seven-hour stretch during the night. Some nights, he still woke up. But he didn't need food. When he woke up, Samantha naturally woke up, too. But she only peeked into the room; she didn't go in. Gabe would turn his face from side to side and cry a little as he settled himself. Then he went back to sleep on his own.

I tell you Gabe's story so that when your little one needs extra time and attention, you'll remind yourself that this will not last forever. If you don't keep this long-term perspective, you're likely to feel overwhelmed, maybe even desperate. And that's when you're in danger of getting into bad habits.

I can't predict when your baby will learn to go to sleep on her own, sleep comfortably, and take less time to be soothed when she wakes up. By the end of this month, she still might not sleep more than a four-hour stretch at night. Still, if you accept that a baby's learning how to settle herself is a process and if you avoid the common sleep pitfalls, I can assure you that you're at least going in the right direction.

Even more important, gas bubbles and nighttime crankiness *will* pass—maybe not as soon as you'd like. However, bad habits will most definitely linger, and undoing them will be very difficult. Rely on the good sleep associations I described earlier. They are easier on you and will teach your baby to soothe himself. Best of all, they are practices that will continue to help him even as he gets older.

Chapter 13

WHO'S TAKING CARE
OF *YOU*, MOM?

What is more challenging than dealing with a crying baby? Even an angelic baby is dependent on you 24/7. It's a little better when you have help, but many women don't. Either way, though, you must take care of yourself. It's like what they say on airplanes: when the oxygen mask drops, put on your own mask first. If you don't, your physical, mental, and emotional self won't be able to handle what's happening.

You, the Basics:
Sleep-Eat-Emotions Plan

You've signed up for an around-the-clock job. In the first month, you're face-to-face with that reality, actually living the experience—waking up every two to three hours in the middle of the night, every four if you're lucky, and wondering how long you can take it, how long you *have* to take it. And if you're breast-feeding, which I hope you are, you probably feel like a "milk machine," as one new mother put it, if not an actual cow! There are four things you can do to take care of yourself: sleep, eat well, monitor your emotions, and plan ahead.

Sleep

As difficult as it might be to imagine as a new mother, you must make time to rest. The first week, you probably slept when your baby slept. Keep it up. If you can't sleep, at least lie down. Granted, caring for yourself when you have a newborn is a challenge. You want to be a good mother, but you feel you still have to run a house, answer calls and emails, and, if you're on maternity leave, field calls from work. Say no to all of the above. Give yourself at least two weeks before you start trying to catch up, longer if you've had a cesarean section—which isn't just childbirth, it's surgery. The world will be there when you're ready for it.

If you're breast-feeding, sleep is also essential to your milk production. If you're giving your baby formula, sleep will make you feel better and improve your mood. You'll have greater pleasure in being with your new baby. You're also more likely to remind yourself that this stage of motherhood lasts a relatively short time.

Eat Well

When you were pregnant, your body stored extra calories that are now used to produce breast milk. Therefore, in the initial months of breast-feeding, your "yield"—how much and what kind of milk you produce—isn't dependent on what you eat. Still, if your diet is inadequate—if you don't consume enough proteins, fats, and carbohydrates or drink enough water—your body will use up those stored calories quickly. You will feel irritated and tired. Not only will that affect your milk production, but you also might become depressed. As a nursing mother, respect your hunger. Consume more snacks and more frequent meals than before you started breast-feeding. Also, drink at least eight cups of water a day.

What you eat can affect your baby, but the link is not as direct as some believe. For example, eating chocolate doesn't make you produce chocolate milk! However, in my experience, I suspect that some babies are affected by their moms' diet. When you eat spicy food or foods that cause adults to feel gassy afterward (beans, cabbage, onions, broccoli, and citrus fruits are some examples), it doesn't necessarily cause your baby discomfort, but why take the chance? Better safe than sorry. It's a simple matter for a breast-feeding mother to eliminate those foods from her diet to see whether it makes a difference.

Clearly, some babies have a higher degree of sensitivity than others—for example, to products derived from cow's milk, such as cheese and yogurt. Chocolate and caffeinated drinks can also be problematic. If your baby suffers from gas, reflux, or colic, it can't hurt to avoid one food type at a time, and wait a few days to see if removing that food eases her discomfort.

The two drink substances I'm most concerned about are caffeine and alcohol. You might not want to hear this, especially if you went without either or both for the last nine months. However, caffeine in great amounts can make your baby irritable. It's OK to have one or two cups of coffee or a soft drink per day if you must.

Alcohol is more serious, as it can be passed on to your baby through your milk. This is a time when your baby's brain is developing. He starts life with about 30 percent of the cerebral cells he will have as an adult. And then, during the next twelve months of his life, 90 percent of his brain will be formed. Because alcohol can interfere with this process, I advise complete abstinence. Why take a risk, knowing that by the time your little one reaches eighteen months, 95 percent of his adult brain will be formed?

Monitor Your Emotions

Being a new mother is an emotional experience, joy mixed with fear! Add a helping of fatigue and raging hormones, and you've got a recipe for mood swings that I described earlier as "baby blues." You might snap at people (often, your husband) or cry a lot. It's best to talk about your feelings and know that they go with your new role. Share them with your husband, a relative, or a friend whom you trust. Talk about your doubts and concerns. Cry when you need to. After all, you're not Superwoman. Most important, get your rest (see above). Ask for and accept help (see below).

Plan Ahead

We all feel saner and safer when we have a plan. It's simple. You know you need to eat. Having healthful prepared meals in the freezer allows you to cross one "to do" item off your list. You feel better when you eat well, keep up your strength, and don't have to spend much time in the kitchen. If you love to cook and feel up to it, it also might be fun for you and your husband to prepare a few meals together. If possible, try to budget for some extra takeout dinners after the baby arrives. It's an expense that will pay itself back by renewing your stamina. If possible, also put work projects on hold, at least for the first six weeks, so that you don't have to split your time, energy, and attention. Trust me, you'll do better if you just take care of the baby and yourself.

Helpers or Invaders?

You might not be able to afford paid help; most women can't. But if you have family, close friends, and good neighbors who are willing to pitch in, that can lighten your load. But beware. Some helpers hit just the right note, lending a hand when asked and (when you're ready) getting you out of the house. Others will feel like invaders. At times, those extra bodies can complicate an already stressful situation.

What happens when Dad changes his first diaper . . . with his mother-in-law hovering over his shoulder? What do you say when your own mother insists that there's a "better" way? What do you do when your entire extended family wants to show up and celebrate? Here are some guidelines that can help.

Limit visitors to almost no one at first. This is not a time for socializing; it's for getting help. The good helpers in your life will understand. Others might be insulted. They don't realize that visits are for you, not for them. Try not to overreact when someone insists on visiting when it's inconvenient for you. Simply say something along these lines: "I love that you're so eager to see the baby, and I hope that we can arrange something soon. But for now, I really have my hands full. So I'd appreciate it if you could give me a few more weeks to settle in." Even when you welcome visitors, excuse yourself when it's time to feed the baby. Both of you need quiet and privacy.

Figure out what you need. Make lists of things to be done, and be specific when you ask others to pitch in. Do you need them to shop, prepare meals, clean, run errands, take care of older children, walk the dog?

Be creative. Will the dry cleaner deliver? If not, can someone else be assigned that job? Can a neighbor help with the dog? Do you know a teenager who can water the garden or clean up the yard?

Tell everyone that when you want advice, you'll ask. Let them know you prefer to discover the wonder of your new baby on your own. Stick to *your* plan. For example, if a visitor protests when you say it's time for baby to go night-night ("But he's smiling; he's not even tired"), say something like: "I know you'd like to hold him longer, but if I don't get him into bed now, he'll get overtired—and then none of us will be smiling!" Don't fall into the trap of trying to explain or defend yourself. This is your baby; you know him best.

Continue to use common sense about protecting your baby. We covered this earlier, but it bears repeating. Tell anyone who's sick to stay away. Your newborn's immune system is not yet fully developed, so if she is exposed to a virus she might not be able to fight infection. If she gets sick, it will interfere with her ability to eat and sleep. And if you get sick, it will be harder to cope and take care of your baby.

Remember that your partner isn't a visitor or an extra "helper." He's the one person you shouldn't have to ask, and if you do, perhaps it's time to read some of this book together, particularly the "Dear Dad/Partner" sidebar in chapter 4.

Getting Out of the House

Your life has changed dramatically. Almost everything is about the baby. When your partner comes home, all you talk about is the baby. Perhaps you already feel a little isolated. And if you don't already know it, in a few weeks, you will realize how hard it is to get out of the house with a new baby. You can't just run out to the store and buy groceries. Everything has to be planned.

It might feel lonely, too. You no longer "speak the same language" as old friends who don't have babies. You don't have much in common with friends who have older children. And on the bad days, when you don't get much sleep, it probably feels as if this phase will never end. You're stuck in a strange, overwhelming lifestyle.

Know that what you're feeling is typical. Even my clients, who have me at their side full-time, feel the same way when they first become mothers. The smart ones do something about it. They leave the house at least once a week. They get back to parts of their routine that they love, whether it's going to the gym (after their doctors say it's OK), to the hairdresser, or to shop. And they seek the company of people they trust.

Be proactive. Make new friends with new mothers you met in childbirth classes or on the maternity ward. Look in your local

HOW TO START YOUR OWN MOMS GROUP

- Find moms with similar interests. It's more important to have babies close in age than it is to have known them before.
- Start small. Keep it to three or four members at first. Keep your goal modest: to share experiences of being first-time mothers.
- Rotate houses. The burden of hosting shouldn't fall on any one person's shoulders.
- Do what works for your group. Be completely unstructured; just meet and see what unfolds. Or focus on a particular subject each week—for example, discuss baby-care philosophies, books, or common problems.
- Talk about your anxieties. After all, you're all going through similar changes. Others can offer you helpful insights, and you can benefit from one another's experiences.
- Set a trial time period, of, say, six to twelve weeks. Then reevaluate. You might want to disband or, as with some of my clients, stay with your group until your kids go to preschool.

paper for listings of Mommy and Me groups and other resources. Community centers and baby stores hoping to attract potential customers often sponsor mothers groups or baby-care classes conducted by professionals. Or, start your own group (see box).

If you don't like the idea of being in a group, at least get yourself out of the house. Weather permitting, walk around your neighborhood and start up conversations with other mothers of babies. Even better, head to the park. Most have child-friendly areas, where you will see other moms, dogs, kids, nannies, and dads. It's not only easy to strike up a conversation in these settings, but watching other (older) children playing will also give you a preview of life to come. And who knows? You also might find a grown-up you enjoy. Some of my best moments and most interesting encounters while caring for babies and toddlers happened in parks around the world.

How Long Will This Time—and These Feelings—Last?

You've become a mother. It's been a month. And in that short time, your life has changed dramatically. You have stepped into a new role, and so much comes with that. You're responsible for another human life, a life that feels as if it is part of you. Motherhood gives you a lot to think about and a lot to do. No wonder you have to take care of yourself.

Whether your first month left you floundering or flew by without a hitch, you know by now that you need a plan. This is what I hope you've learned from me this month: life goes better when you have a good routine that allows time for *your* physical and emotional needs, and how well you take care of your baby is how well you take care of yourself—not only now, in your child's infancy, but for all the months and years hereafter.

Again, try to keep a long-term perspective. You won't be as tired or as stressed out as you are now. You will eventually sleep better, and your baby will learn to do things on her own. This time will fly by. In fact, your little one will go off to school before you know it. Mothering is a long and hard job. But if you have a good routine, continue to take care of *you*, and keep your eye out for what's down the road, you'll be able to meet the challenges along the way.

Notes on the First Month

Look How Much My Baby Grew!

My baby weighs _____ pounds, which is _____ more/less than he weighed at birth.

My baby measures _____ inches, which is _____ "taller" than he was at birth.

Eat

Write down your memories of feeding your baby. What did you feed—breast milk, formula, or both—and how often? What was easy or difficult? How did you feel when you were nursing or giving your baby a bottle?

_____

_____

_____

_____

Play

How long could your baby stay up after a feeding? What seemed to amuse her most: Your face? A sibling? A painting? Looking out the window or at a book?

_____

_____

_____

_____

Sleep

What was your baby's early sleep pattern like? Did he drift off to sleep easily or need your help to calm down? What worked best? What did he look like when he was trying to settle himself to sleep? What kinds of sounds did he make?

_____

_____

_____

_____

What Else Is Happening?

Here, add any other observations or thoughts about your baby's second month:

_____

_____

_____

_____

OUR ROUTINE

It's important to keep track of your baby's day at this point. I've provided the hours; you fill in the minutes, so you'll have a good sense of when your baby eats, plays, and sleeps. If her routine is rarely consistent, you might want to make copies of this page and keep track for several days in a row.

5: _____

6: _____

7: _____

8: _____

9: _____

10: _____

11: _____

12: _____

1: _____

2: _____

3: _____

4: _____

5: _____

6: _____

7: _____

8: _____

9: _____

10: _____

11: _____

12: _____

1: _____

2: _____

3: _____

4: _____

PHASE IV

The Second Month:
Are We Having Fun Yet?

IN A NUTSHELL

Depending on your baby and how you've handled her so far, you will start seeing the early signs that she's moving toward a good routine. For some mothers, then, the second month brings a sigh of relief. For others, it can be tricky, because now is the time when we try to encourage independent play and sleep.

COVERED IN THIS PHASE

Adjusting the eat-play-sleep routine

The difficult-to-calm baby

How are we doing?

*Y*our baby is growing up, just starting to smile, and becoming more of a presence in the household. Mom, you're still the one she looks for, but now she also responds to other familiar faces, especially people in your household who cuddle and coo at her.

By now, breast-feeding is well established. If you formula-feed, you've probably figured out which type and brand are best. Even if you have to veer from a consistent feeding routine on the weekend or when unexpected events happen, you return to it quickly. Your baby loves her bath and massage. When she cries, you know how to calm her.

The sleep part of your routine is going well, too. Most mornings, your baby is cheery or easily calmed once you take him from his crib. Most nights, after his relaxing bath and massage ritual, you put him to bed with little or no crying. He's getting better at going to sleep without your help, but his naps are still uneven. Sometimes he sleeps for a good stretch and, other times, only for a half hour or forty-five minutes. Still, you're getting better at "reading" what he needs.

Wait! That's not what's happening in your household? You've had trouble establishing a routine? Your baby's eating is still erratic? He often spits up? He cries a lot? If so, there's a good chance that he spent a lot of the first month in your arms or with someone else holding and trying to comfort him. Or maybe he's most comfortable in the baby swing or when being driven in a car. Your pediatrician keeps assuring you that "it's normal" and "he'll grow out of it," but you're not so sure. You try to keep your baby comfortable, but some days it's hard to believe it's ever going to get better.

If that last paragraph describes your circumstances, you might have a difficult-to-calm baby. So while some people are having fun by the time their babies reach the second month, you might not be. Your baby might still be crying a lot before he finally goes to sleep. Or perhaps it's impossible for you to leave him alone, because he already depends on you and other members of your household to entertain him.

How your second month goes depends on which situation you're in. If things are going smoothly, you're ready to move along. If not, you probably have to correct course.

Chapter 14

ADJUSTING THE ROUTINE:

EAT, PLAY, SLEEP

One of the challenges now is to start teaching the newest member of your family how to amuse and soothe himself without your help. This means that there will be small, subtle changes in his routine: more feedings during the day, more playtime. It's also important to pay attention to your baby's sleep habits, his temperament, and how you've been responding to him so far. Perhaps he can be weaned off swaddling. Let's start by looking at the basics and what, ideally, you're moving toward in the second month.

Eat: More During the Day

Babies who go long periods without eating during the day make up for the lost nutrition by wanting to eat more at night. So one goal in the second month is to try to get your little one to eat more during the day. You do this by feeding her at approximately three-hour intervals. This can be challenging. Beginning around the second month, your baby—now more aware of her environment—might get distracted and stop eating. Try not to talk to her during a feeding. Otherwise, she might stop before her tummy is full and become hungry less than three hours later. On the other hand, if she eats too fast, it's a good idea to encourage her to slow down by burping her in the middle of the feeding.

How much breast milk or formula will your baby consume? It depends in part on how big she is. Big babies naturally eat more than small babies. But we also tend to overfeed, because we fear that the baby is not full. If you're breast-feeding, your body will manufacture what you need. You can ensure this by drinking a lot of water or herbal tea and getting plenty of rest. If you're formula-feeding, and she sucks vigorously on the bottle until there's no more milk left, give her a half-ounce more at the next feeding. I prefer to stop at six ounces unless a baby is unusually large. Remember that your baby's tummy is the size of *her* fist, not yours.

When a mom complains to me that her baby is not eating much during the day, I ask two questions:

> › How often does he nurse or take a bottle during the day?

> › How far apart are his feedings?

Earlier, in the "Notes on the First Month," I suggested that you keep track of your baby's feedings (as well as sleep and play periods), so that you'd have this information on hand. Perhaps it felt like too big a job. But if you can't answer those questions, it means that now is the time to start. It will pay off.

Spacing feedings out to occur every three hours encourages your baby to consume more during the day. But you also have to be flexible. If your baby seems very hungry, it's OK to feed him up to thirty minutes earlier. But as you move through the day, try to adjust fifteen minutes here, a half hour there, if possible, so that bedtime feedings are always at the same time, ideally around seven to seven thirty P.M.

Eating regularly during the day will also help your baby sleep better and, eventually, eat less at night. Once she weighs fourteen pounds, usually around three or four months old, she won't need those nighttime feedings for nutrition. At that point, you will slowly decrease the amount of milk you offer her, giving her body time to adjust to sleeping on less milk.

Most of the babies in my care have two feedings during the night at this age, one before I go to bed, around eleven P.M., and another at, say, two A.M. I've found that infants who eat well during the day often stop wanting night feedings on their own. In some cases, though, they then begin to wake up at around five A.M. As I advised earlier, always wait a few minutes before rushing in. Believe me, Mom, it's easier to break this pattern now than when he is four or five months old. If you need to feed him, do so, but only after giving him a few minutes alone to cry or go back to sleep. You'll probably also have to change his diaper, but don't talk or make a fuss over him. In other words, act as if it's still nighttime. He will probably go back to sleep.

Play = Growth Time

Last month, your baby's playtime was brief and was more about making contact, not really about play. The idea was to connect with her and put a "space" between feeding and sleep so that she didn't get into the habit of sleeping immediately after eating. In the second month, however, playtime is more about stimulating her senses and gradually "training" her to amuse herself. She can stay up longer now, an hour to ninety minutes after a feeding. By the time she's three months old, she will last for two hours.

Be sure to alternate positions during each play period. She might spend some of it in your arms, some in an infant carrier, some in a little baby seat, and some on the floor, both on her back and on her tummy. For example, you might first put her on the floor under a Gymini. If you don't have one, no problem. Arrange colorful objects around her on the floor, so she has something to look at. Initially, she will just stare. Then she'll make jerky movements, as if she's trying to reach for whatever is in her line of sight. Later, she will try to touch her toys and, eventually, grab them and actually play with them.

For a change of scene and position, put her in her baby chair so she can watch out the window, gaze at a ceiling fan, or watch whatever you're doing. If she gets bored, gently shake a baby toy to distract her. I also like to start reading now. She won't understand, but she'll enjoy sitting on your lap, looking at the pictures, and hearing the sound of your voice.

If you haven't already begun to give your baby tummy time, place him on his belly for at least part of the play period. He might not like it at first, but gradually keep it up, for a few minutes during every playtime. To make it more inviting, lie on the floor, facing him. This position stimulates him and builds strength in his neck and back muscles. It gets his body ready for crawling later on. Little by little, your baby will get used to the position, and he'll benefit by seeing the world from a new vantage point.

It is very important to look your baby in the eye and "talk" face-to-face. You're teaching him to make eye contact, which is the beginning of communication and helps your baby's developing brain. You'll notice that he is, in his own way, interacting. He gets excited, moves his arms and legs in response, and smiles. His eyes light up when you talk to him. He'll start to "talk" to you with little coos and goo-goos and, at around four or five months old, laughter.

Even though at this age, your baby isn't capable of actually playing much, keep reminding yourself that everyone learns by doing. Sometimes I see adults playing *for* the baby instead of letting the baby do it himself. We adults already know how to play, right? So give your baby lots of opportunities to explore and to manipulate toys on his own. Of course, at times, you will show him how something works. But then let him take over.

Playtime is also when Dad, siblings, grandparents, relatives, and friends get to know the baby and spend time with her without disrupting feedings or naps. Play acquaints your baby with the social structure of the family. Let others hold the baby and interact with her. Encourage everyone to engage in centuries-old, silly, melodic baby talk. This might seem pointless with such a young baby, because she's certainly not capable of answering. But it will teach her, even at this age, how to be a social person.

Playtime is an opportunity to be with your baby *and* to teach him how to amuse himself. Make sure you do a little of both, so that he doesn't get the idea that the only way to be happy is to have Mommy or another adult entertaining him. Babies don't necessarily like to be alone; independent play is something they learn. So after about ten minutes of playing with him, if he seems content, move out of his line of sight. Let him discover his surroundings. Left on his own, he'll distract himself. Step in only when he gets bored or needs a change of scene or position.

In my years of working with children, I have learned that when babies learn to amuse themselves, they become more self-sufficient and creative, even as toddlers. They also become better sleepers, because when they don't drift off immediately, instead of crying, they know how to distract themselves. Of course, I also take care to leave the baby in safe conditions.

How do you know when it's OK to increase playtime and when to end it? By watching your baby! Gradually, you will notice that your baby can last longer, that he's happy just to look around. You will know when it's time to end playtime and wind down when your baby begins to make "tired" signs; he might yawn, rub his eyes, or get a bit fussy. Stop playtime and pick him up *before* he cries. Check his diaper, and get ready to put him to sleep. Close the shades to differentiate playtime from sleeptime.

Sleep: The End of Swaddling?

One change in the sleep routine this month is that some babies don't need to be confined during sleep. They no longer make reflexive twitching movements as they're drifting off or when asleep. So we gradually start teaching them to sleep unswaddled. To be sure, swaddling an infant marks the end of the play period. And it's an especially invaluable sleep aid when your baby is new to the world. When swaddled, no arms or legs flail above him, so he goes to sleep more comfortably and is more likely to stay asleep. I don't blame you for wanting to keep it up.

But as with all sleep aids, we have to play attention to changes in the baby. As she gets older, restricting your baby's movement at night might affect her motor development. I stop swaddling babies when the twitching reflexes start to disappear. Usually, this happens around six weeks, and then it takes me another two weeks to gradually ease off swaddling altogether.

But it also depends on *your* baby. I've swaddled difficult-to-calm babies as long as four months, because immobilizing those flailing arms and legs seems to soothe them. If your little one falls into any of the following categories, you might want to keep swaddling her for another month or two:

› She has trouble settling down.

› She is plagued by tummy troubles.

> She is extremely sensitive.

> When you attempt to teach her to sleep unswaddled (see below), her sleep is disturbed.

Teaching Your Baby to Sleep Unswaddled

If you followed my advice from day one, your baby has learned to sleep swaddled; it makes her feel cozy and secure. To get her used to sleeping unswaddled, proceed slowly, allowing her to get used to having her body free while sleeping.

First, release one arm. That is, when you wrap her, leave one arm out of the swaddling. If she can't fall asleep or wakes up frequently, swaddle her fully, wait a week, and try to leave one arm out again. Wait even longer, if necessary.

When she seems completely comfortable having one arm free, start to experiment with both arms out of the swaddling. If she is able to get to sleep on her own, with a minimum of crying, great.

Wait another week, or longer, to stop swaddling altogether. You can also transition her to a sleep sack, which isn't as confining as swaddling but will still give her a sense of being "encased" while she sleeps.

Once your baby begins to sleep unswaddled, pay attention to the temperature of her room to make sure that she's not cold at night. Babies do not use covers, and when they sleep, their body temperature drops. If your baby gets cold in the middle of the night, she will start to move her limbs in an attempt to warm up. That movement will wake her, and she'll cry. This is less likely to happen if she's in warm pajamas or a sleep sack. If possible, you can also adjust the temperature of her room.

Naps: An Ongoing Challenge

Around the second month, as awake time starts to extend, sleep is more important than ever. A well-rested baby is a happy baby. It is *not* true that keeping a baby up during the day makes him sleep at night. Naps keep your little one rested and calm during the day and also better able to sleep at night.

It's great for a baby to have good naps during the day, but in my experience, many babies don't. This is a common source of frustration for mothers. Erratic naps make it difficult to plan your day. Ironically, your baby has trouble napping now, in part because you take him out more than you did during the first month. You take walks, do errands, take him to lunch, and he has two new options for napping: the carriage or the car seat. When he gets tired, the movement soothes him, and he falls asleep easily. Even as he goes in and out of REM—the lighter sleep cycle that occurs approximately every forty-five minutes—the motion puts him back to sleep. On outings with you, therefore, he is likely to sleep for an hour or more, especially if you're taking a long walk or car ride.

The real problem is that he gets used to falling asleep in motion, which is something the crib can't do. It doesn't move or rock. So when you put him down for a nap at home, he falls asleep for a while. But at the end of each sleep cycle, he wakens and doesn't know how to put himself back to sleep. He wakes up and stays up.

Honestly, there's not much you can do about too-short naps at this age. But we can try to head in the right direction. Even though you love being out and about with your baby, have him take at least one nap a day in his own crib.

Be consistent. Prepare your baby for naps the way you do for bedtime: quiet time, blinds down, room dark, swaddling or half-swaddling. A bedtime ritual, repeated over and over, lets your baby know that naptime is coming. Put him into his crib awake, and leave the room. Then cross your fingers and hope. Some babies are good sleepers right from the beginning, but many have trouble with naps.

Again, it depends on your baby. A forty-five-minute nap in the morning might be OK, enough to "hold" him until his next feeding without him getting overtired. But forty-five minutes in the afternoon is rarely enough. Chances are, he'll spend the rest of the day cranky. A tired baby doesn't eat well. He gets overtired and tends to sleep through meals. He skips playtime. It's a bad pattern, one that I often have to deal with on the job. Here's what I do.

If the baby wakes up after forty-five minutes of napping, encourage him to go back to sleep. Go to him, soothe him, and put a pacifier in his mouth. It might not work. At that point, I simply put the baby on my belly or chest and take a nap *with* him.

I can hear you saying, "But you said not to hold the baby to sleep." Yes, that's right. But the idea is to let him be on his own when he is OK and help him when necessary. Babies at this age don't know how to put themselves back to sleep. For a while, you have to help them learn how. On some days, sleep rituals won't be enough to calm your baby. He might be having a rough time of it—say, because of tummy problems or a cold. Sometimes providing the right conditions for sleep includes holding him. You have to forget the routine on those days and help him feel better.

Do not worry; your baby is not going to get used to sleeping on you. And we're only doing this for a short time. When things get back to normal, you can go back to your routine. Also, your baby will not be so easily roused as he gets older. What you want is for him to get used to a pattern of sleeping longer.

If your baby requires more cuddling and holding at this age, use the time to bond with him. Sometimes he will go back to sleep, and you'll both get some much-needed rest. Other times, though, he won't. Again, I remind you to keep it in perspective. It might feel as if you've been at this forever, but this is only your second month together!

With all my years of experience, I have learned that when you have a goal, you have to keep working toward it. That is exactly what we are doing here, gradually helping your baby extend his naps. Trust me, down the road, if you don't give up, he will get used to longer naps and you won't have to think about it anymore.

If your baby has been taking short naps since birth and hasn't had even one long stretch of sleeping during the day, you might need to look at his *overall* sleep routine. Perhaps you already sense that he's a "bad sleeper." If so, go back to the basics. Review my sleep routine in chapter 12. If you're still having trouble, he might be a difficult-to-calm baby. If so, chapter 15 will help you understand him better.

WHAT IF . . . My Baby Sleeps During the Day and Wakes Up at Night?

Babies don't know the difference between day and night. We have to teach them by keeping them on a steady feeding routine and by making sure they get playtime. We don't let them sleep longer than four hours during the day and never let them skip a daytime feeding. When we go into the nursery at night, we do what we have to, but we don't talk to them. We want to discourage them from being up when it's dark out.

We also try to give them more food at the end of the day. Some babies respond well to having an extra feeding in the afternoon or evening. If you're breast-feeding, your milk supply is lower at the end of the day, so try to feed your baby before the bath and massage and, afterward, give her a "top-off" before bedtime. Gradually, she will begin to space the night feedings farther apart. But as we will see in the next chapter, being well fed during the day is not the only factor in a baby sleeping through the night.

Chapter 15

THE DIFFICULT-TO-CALM BABY

A few years ago I was hired by Maggie, a new mom who needed around-the-clock help with her twins, Seth and Janna. Maggie, a prosecutor, was a smart, take-charge woman, but neither her success nor her strength prepared her for the challenge of new motherhood. Granted, she had twins, but it was more than that. In fact, one of them, Janna, was an angel, one of the easiest babies I have ever seen. Good thing, too, because her brother, Seth, cried as much and as long as any baby I have ever cared for. His sister slept peacefully in her crib, but Seth went to bed upright, in his car seat.

The twins were on breast milk, supplemented by formula. Now, you might wonder if the formula was to blame for Seth's discomfort, but Janna was ingesting the same formula, and she was fine. I tried everything—feeding him slowly, burping him longer than his sister. After he ate, if he cried, I'd put him on my lap, facedown, and massage his back gently in a clockwise motion. I "bicycled" his little legs. I walked around with him in the baby carrier. But he still cried.

No one could figure out what was wrong with him. Seth was

gaining weight and growing. He was alert and could follow an object with his eyes. He jumped, appropriately, at sudden noises. Therefore, the pediatrician said Seth was healthy. Besides, crying is part of every baby's life, right? His excessive crying, the doctor suggested, could be caused by "colic," a word pediatricians often use to describe babies who cry a lot for no apparent reason. He assured Maggie that some infants go through bouts of discomfort. They would go away. "If the hard crying doesn't ease up by the time he's three months old," he added, "we will talk again."

Some people might call Seth a "difficult" baby. I prefer to think of him as a "difficult-to-calm" baby. If you have a baby like Seth, you know it's not his fault. He's not being difficult on purpose! He is uncomfortable or in pain and doesn't know how to cope with it, except to cry. He deserves your compassion.

You probably have a difficult-to-calm baby if you . . .

› have to spend a lot of time holding and comforting her.

› almost always have trouble getting her to sleep.

› make frequent calls and visits to the pediatrician.

› think of her as "difficult" or "a crier."

› feel as if you've "tried everything" and "nothing works."

› are totally exhausted because she requires constant care day and night.

If you read this book before your baby arrived, you might have wondered, *Is my baby going to be that way?* Chances are, no. Only about 10 to 20 percent of the babies I've cared for cry excessively and are difficult to calm. Most babies are much easier.

If you do have a difficult-to-calm baby, remember that your love for her can do much more than you imagine. You adore this little creature of yours so much that all you care about is minimizing her discomfort. In fact, in my experience, mothers of difficult-to-calm babies get even more attached, because they spend so much time with their children.

Why Do They Cry So Much?

In one sense, I agree with little Seth's pediatrician. Some babies cry a lot, the reason isn't always clear, and the best you can do is ride it out. You try all the "tricks" that calm most babies. And sometimes they help . . . for a little while.

The only way to keep Seth comfortable, we finally realized, was to hold him a lot during the day. We had no choice but to let him sleep in his car seat. We had tried everything else—raising the crib at one end, having him sleep in a swing, and letting him sleep in a vibrating baby seat—but his car seat was the only place Seth was comfortable enough to fall asleep.

We knew he couldn't sleep in the car seat forever. So from time to time, we'd try putting him into his crib. At first, he couldn't tolerate it for more than a few minutes. Still, we kept trying, little by little, day by day. Getting through those early months of continual crying and comforting was very hard on Maggie. But our persistence paid off.

By the time he was four months old, Seth could fall asleep in his crib and stay asleep for more than an hour. He often woke up in the middle of the night and had to be comforted. But at one year old, he was sleeping as well as his sister. In all that time, no one could pinpoint exactly why he was so difficult to calm. Looking at the twins today, I'd guess that it was in part Seth's personality; he's still less agreeable and social than his sister. And he still has a sensitive stomach. I wouldn't be surprised if he developed allergies, too.

Some infants cry a lot during the first few days because they're hungry. It can take up to three or four days for Mom's milk to come in completely. Or the baby himself has feeding difficulties, as we discussed earlier. However, by the second month, most difficult-to-calm babies have other challenges, sometimes more than one.

Digestive issues. Gas, colic, and/or reflux usually begin late in the first month and are most intense by the second month. These are three different conditions (although all three can be labeled "colic"). However, all three cause discomfort and pain, which is why these babies tend to cry a lot.

Sensitivity. Whether it's because of their low birth weight or inborn temperament, some babies are easily upset by what's happening in their environment—noise, light, touch, new experiences. Their reaction is to cry.

Allergies. Babies can be allergic to their mothers' milk or to certain brands of formula. They can have a reaction to their mothers' diet. Or they can be allergic to something in the environment, such as trees or mold. The discomfort, regardless of the reason, causes these babies to complain in the only way they can: by crying.

Temperament. Some infants are more active and move more than others. Some are more reactive and more easily upset. Eventually, they can learn how to manage their emotions and mood swings, but in the meantime, they balk or cry a lot.

Illness. Babies cry when they're uncomfortable or in pain. Anything from the common cold to a more serious condition can make them miserable and hard to console.

If your baby cries a lot and is hard to soothe for any of the above reasons, by all means consult your pediatrician. However, many mothers of difficult-to-calm babies are told what Maggie was told: Wait it out. Do your best to calm her in the meantime. Of course, in this book, I can't diagnose your baby, either. I don't know her. But I can offer you some important points to help you get through the hard times, as Maggie did:

> Regardless of the reason, difficult-to-calm babies do require more time, care, and patience. Hunker down, and expect that you will be busy soothing your baby during the first months.

> Don't compare your baby's progress to that of other babies, and don't "wish" that he was different. He is who he is.

> Although it feels as if there's no end in sight, you won't be dealing with this forever. In some cases, your baby will "grow out of," or heal from, whatever condition he has. Even when you're dealing with temperament, which is part of who your baby is, you will come to know him, learn how to handle him, and structure your environment to teach and protect him.

> Difficult-to-calm babies benefit from routine, too. In fact, they need routine even more than most babies. The trouble is, it often can be tough to stick to a routine with a difficult-to-calm baby. That, of course, doesn't mean you should stop trying.

Does the "Why" Really Matter?

Although I always insist that my clients consult their pediatricians about excessive crying, even with a professional's guidance, it's sometimes not clear why a baby is miserable. For example, "colic" is often used as an umbrella term for any type of discomfort. It's true that tummyaches often play a big part in babies' discomfort, so it's not a bad guess. At the same time, there are other possible digestive issues, so the picture gets clouded and complicated. Also, some babies have more than one issue.

Gas, which can start at any time, is most common. If your baby pulls his legs up to his chest, if he cries after a feeding, and if it's hard to comfort him, it might be gas. Gas pains get worse when your baby ingests milk. However, it can bother your baby at any time of day, not just after meals but also during play or in the middle of a nap. You'll see his little body tense up as the gas bubbles start forming and pressing against his insides. Before you know it, he's awake, screaming. Fortunately, gas pains usually peak around six weeks. They're common but also worrisome, because you're not sure whether something more serious is going on.

Reflux is usually accompanied by excessive spitting up and crying. Because nursing or ingesting formula too fast can make it worse, burp your baby a few times during each feeding. If you (or your pediatrician) suspect reflux, it's also good to diaper your baby before nursing him. After a feeding, lying on a flat surface will make it more difficult for him to digest. As with an adult who has heartburn, the milk will come up (and sometimes out), which can be very painful. If you have to change his diaper when his stomach is full, try not to keep him flat for too long. Raise his legs only slightly, and slip the diaper under him without lifting his back off the changing table. After a daytime feeding, when you move into playtime, wait a half hour before laying him down on his back or stomach. In the meantime, you can put him in his baby seat. After his seven P.M. feeding—usually, the last before bedtime—hold him upright for at least twenty minutes. When you lay him down, elevate his head by placing towels or a folded blanket under the head end of his mattress. (Be sure to place them across the entire width of the mattress, from side to side; otherwise, he might accidentally roll over.)

With *colic*, your baby will tend to suffer at the same time each day, and it is unrelenting. No one knows what causes colic, although the symptoms often include gas and vomiting, just like reflux.

As your baby becomes more mature and can better tolerate breast milk or formula, he will probably suffer less from gas, reflux, or colic, which usually disappear by the end of the third or fourth month—sometimes later, depending on the baby.

Any of these digestive issues can also set in motion a vicious cycle. The discomfort makes it hard for a baby to get to sleep on his own. Pain often disrupts sleep, too. So he ends up being over-tired, and that makes him cry even more. In addition, although digestive issues are common, as I mentioned earlier, they're not the only reason babies cry a lot. The problem is that at two months, a more sophisticated diagnosis is impossible.

Harrison's story is a perfect example. He and his parents lived in a beautiful home in Beverly Hills, surrounded by lush gardens and trees. Poor little dear, he cried every day at the end of the day, and no one—not his pediatrician or the endocrine specialist his parents later consulted—knew exactly why. He was, everyone finally concluded, a "colicky" baby.

During one doctor visit, Harrison started to cry, but I managed to comfort him. While his mom was talking to the doctor, I held Harrison upright, his face on my chest. Feeling my heart beat calmed him a bit. I laid my free hand on his back and started "trotting" around the office, walking with an up-and-down motion.

"I can see that he cries," said the doctor, noticing also that Harrison was settling down, "but his crying is obviously manageable."

We spent the next month or so consoling Harrison—holding him, calming him, distracting him from his discomfort. The mother chose not to give him the pain medication the pediatrician had recommend; she tried homeopathic drops instead.

Eventually, Harrison cried less, but when he was around two, he sometimes had trouble breathing. A new doctor discovered why: Harrison had asthma. As it turned out, he was allergic to the mold that had formed on his bedroom wall. Outside his window, a dense group of trees blocked the sunlight, which prevented the dampness from drying out after a rainstorm.

I suspect that Harrison's asthma attacks didn't just start when he was two years old. He was always allergic to the mold, but at two months it was diagnosed as colic. How could his first doctors have missed this? How could they have just called it colic? It happens every day, because when very young babies are uncomfortable, the only thing adults usually see is the baby crying.

Of course, you should seek professional help for any infant who cries a lot. But know that the advice you get might or might not be effective with a difficult-to-calm baby. And it might not be the whole story. Your doctor might recommend changes, such as switching to a different brand of formula or elevating one end of the crib.

Work with your pediatrician; bring him or her all the information you have. Pay attention. Is there a time when the crying usually occurs? Does it happen in a particular place in the house or outside? Do allergies run in your family? Be your own diagnostician; make an educated guess, and test it out. For example, if allergies run in your family, it would make sense to be more careful about what goes into your baby's crib and what lotions you use on her. If your doctor suggests medication, ask about the side effects and risks. You might feel frustrated and desperate for a solution, but even the best specialist might need to wait until your baby's system is more mature in order to correctly analyze and diagnose what's going on.

I now keep an eye out for signs of undiagnosed allergies, because so many difficult-to-calm babies seem to be affected. Once I was caring for a sweet baby named Bethany, who from the beginning had trouble adjusting to her mother's milk. She also developed jaundice and had phototherapy at home. Her skin was back to normal a week later, but the crying continued. I began to notice, though, that whenever I took Bethany outside, she rarely cried. My guess was that something *in* the house was making it hard for her to breathe. We decided to vacuum her room more, buy her hypoallergenic sheets, and clear her crib of stuffed animals and anything else that could collect dust. Bethany's crying didn't disappear altogether, but it was not quite as intense.

I was lucky that my theory helped in Bethany's case, but sometimes you run out of ideas. At that point, you just have to accept that for approximately the next three or four months, some crying, maybe a lot of crying, will be part of your baby's life.

Calming Your Baby

Just because we don't know why a baby is fretful or in pain, that doesn't mean we can't comfort her. It's hard, and a lot of guesswork is involved, but after all these years, I've discovered that certain strategies help relieve the stress. When I'm with a difficult-to-calm baby, these are the points I try to keep in mind.

Hold him a lot. A difficult-to-calm baby, regardless of the reason for his discomfort, requires more holding. When a baby is continually distressed, he cannot relax on his back, in his crib, or under his Gymini. He will cry, kick, and flail his arms and legs, because he's in pain and can't "say" it any other way. At times like these, there is nothing to do but hold and comfort him.

At this point, as long as your baby weighs eight pounds or more, feel free to use a baby carrier. It is difficult to hold a baby for long periods of time. A carrier presses your baby close to your chest, keeps him upright, and distributes his weight onto your shoulders. He gets the comfort of feeling close to you, and you get a break from holding him.

Keep her upright after feedings. To burp her, make sure that her body is fairly straight, with her head up. Hold her this way for at least twenty minutes to give her an opportunity to expel any air she swallowed during feeding and for her food to digest. Some babies burp right away; others never burp, even when held for a long time. At least, being upright might help ease her discomfort. If she spits up or starts to fuss when you try to put her in her crib, pick her up again. And guess what? *Now* she burps. Why? Because when she's lying down, it's impossible to expel the air that has been trapped in her tummy, a result of gulping down formula or breast milk. When you pick her up, it can come out. Now hold her for another ten minutes or so before laying her down on her back in the bassinet or crib.

Distract him. Sleep aids, such as white noise, soft music, or nature sounds, can also be used to distract a baby from pain. Some babies respond well to the up-and-down movement of "trotting." Others like their backs rubbed in an upward motion. Experiment with what works best with your baby. I've seen parents get very creative: they take babies for walks, drive them in the car, invest in vibrating chairs, bounce on an exercise ball, go up and down a staircase—all in the name of soothing and distracting. I make no judgments, because I know how hard it is to distract a crying baby. As long as the strategy is safe and manages to calm your baby, who am I to say it's wrong, especially after you've tried everything else? I would advise that if the staircase maneuver works, be very careful. Use the handrail, and travel up and down only the two or three bottom steps.

Give her extra sucking time. When in pain, babies look for something to suck on, which is why I like pacifiers at this age. However, even though your baby knows how to suck on a pacifier, she might spit it out when you try to use it to calm her down. Don't assume that she doesn't want it. She's just crying too hard or is too agitated to figure out how to suck on it at that moment.

You can help her by exerting gentle pressure on the pacifier to keep it in her mouth. If she keeps refusing the pacifier, let her suck on your pinkie for a while just to calm her. Then try the pacifier again. Most babies will take it at that point and feel comforted by the sucking.

Take precautions against allergies. Especially if someone in your family had or still fights allergies, your baby's inconsolable cries could be a reaction to something in his environment. Even if it isn't, it makes sense to pay attention. Remove stuffed animals and bookshelves, both big dust collectors, from the baby's room. Be careful to vacuum and dust areas of the house where you're likely to put your baby—carpets, curtains, and shelves in the living room or den and, of course, the nursery. Keep pets out of the nursery for a few days to see if your baby cries less. Stop the use of chemical-based home cleaning products; use water and vinegar to clean floors and surfaces instead. Buy unscented baby products. Check air-conditioner filters.

Continue to swaddle. Sleep is the biggest problem for difficult-to-calm babies. Most infants are disturbed by their own twitching movements, but these babies, who are more sensitive than most, get really upset. As I noted earlier, two months is a good time to teach some babies to sleep unswaddled. But if you have a difficult-to-calm baby, hold off for another month or even two. Swaddling can ease a baby's discomfort or relieve his pain and make it easier for him to sleep.

Will these ideas work all the time? Maybe, and maybe not. But I've found that the combination of holding your baby upright, comforting her, giving her something to suck on, distracting her, and swaddling her usually helps ease the discomfort. Have compassion for her. Resign yourself that it's going to take effort to get through this month with your difficult-to-calm baby.

It's also important to remember that if your baby's crying is the result of a combination of issues, each one affects the others. Let's say you have a baby like Jake. His mother was very high-strung. She was an avid exerciser, always on a diet, always afraid of not being "in shape." I have no idea how her personality or lifestyle affected her pregnancy or what genes she passed on to him, but it's all part of the mix. Jake was low weight at birth, a fussy, inefficient eater right from the beginning, sensitive to noise. It didn't really surprise me that Jake also had tummy issues or that his pediatrician and his mother called him a "colicky" baby. Jake's situation was complex; it involved personality, and who knows what else? Perhaps today he also has allergies. But when I knew him as an infant, it was hard to be more specific.

The point is, unless there's an underlying illness that can be treated, the "why" really doesn't matter. If a baby cries a lot and can't be easily consoled, it's still our job to help him with compassion. It's not his fault, so we just comfort him.

Calming Yourself

If you remain calm yourself, the strategies above are more likely to work. But that can be a tall order. Few things are more challenging than dealing with a baby who cries a lot and whom you can't console. It can be overwhelming to a new mom, more so if you are parenting alone. Throughout the day, make sure that you take care of yourself. If possible, get others to pitch in, or at least get some fresh air and exercise, or do an activity just for you. Most important, take a break when you can no longer tolerate the crying.

From time to time, we hear about adults losing control when babies cry loudly and without interruption. Fortunately, this is uncommon. But such stories should be a warning. If you're starting to get stressed out, and no one else can take over, make a careful exit for a few minutes. It's better for your baby to be crying in her crib than to be in your arms at that moment and sense your agitation.

Before you leave her alone, make sure that the crib is free of blankets, pillows, and toys. Once you leave the room, check on her every ten minutes. At some point, your baby will stop crying, or you will regain enough self-control to tend to her again.

Let me be clear. As a rule, I don't advise leaving babies alone to cry. However, we are all human, and I know firsthand how hard it is to care for a very fussy baby. These babies deserve our compassion and a willingness to put aside our own needs. If you or whoever is in charge can't do that and is starting to lose control, I much prefer to see a crying baby out of reach.

To calm yourself, do some light exercise—say, a few yoga poses. Make yourself a cup of tea or coffee, and try to regain control of your emotions. If you feel insecure, stressed, or ashamed, reach inside yourself, and remember that this is not your fault—some infants *are* more difficult than others—and it won't last forever. Let your maternal love carry you for these next few months. As you gain confidence and know what you're doing, the work will become easier. When we see the results, even if it's hard and even when the results don't show up right away, it's easier to keep at it.

Keep Trying, Despite the Crying

All babies, from those who rarely cry to the most difficult to calm, benefit from having a well-organized life. In the case of Maggie's twins, whom you met at the beginning of this chapter, Janna, the angelic baby, was content for the most part. Nevertheless, she still needed a predictable routine. So we fed her more or less every three hours, waking her rather than letting her sleep through. We made sure that she had a little playtime after feeding, so that she never learned to associate eating with sleeping. We gave her sleep aids—a soft bunny, a mobile over the crib—that helped distract her and gave her a chance to self-soothe. With us helping her organize her days and nights and getting her used to the eat-play-sleep pattern, she never lost that wonderful disposition.

Her brother, Seth, the difficult-to-calm baby, slept for shorter periods than Janna and usually woke up crying. He almost always cried after feedings and sometimes spit up. He needed to be consoled a lot of the time. We often had to hold him until he fell asleep. At times, the minute we tried to put him down in his crib, he woke up, missing the feeling of a warm adult body. Sometimes Seth cried because it was his nature, other times because of tummy troubles—we were never sure. He felt calm only in certain positions. We discovered that he slept better when the head end of the mattress was lifted a little bit and that he liked to "ride" in his baby carrier. He, more than his sister, needed to be in an upright position and close to a beating heart.

As different as they were as babies (by the way, they're still different), Janna and Seth both needed the consistency and predictability of a routine. Getting there was obviously more of a challenge with Seth. Certainly, his crying disrupted our attempts to establish a routine, because it was hard for him to settle. If you have a difficult-to-calm baby like Seth, though, it's important to remember that other factors also matter, factors that *you* can change.

You feel sorry for your baby. All infants should be held a lot. Those who need extra comforting are held much longer and more often. Babies get used to that comfort and to being held almost all the time. And moms get used to giving it. But it's equally important to teach your baby other forms of soothing.

Your baby doesn't have an opportunity to soothe himself. Some babies need more holding, but every baby also needs to learn how to soothe herself when she's going to sleep. Of course, you should hold your baby when she cries. You should also hold her during playtime. But when it's time for bed, after you've settled and swaddled her, the moment she is calm—even if it's just for a very short period—you should put her into her crib. For a fussy baby who has gotten used to being held much of the time, a predictable routine will, little by little, teach her how to soothe and entertain herself.

You're exhausted. It isn't easy to think about any kind of structure when most of your day is spent dealing with a crying baby and, worse, not knowing what's going on or what to do next. I can understand your frustration. Few parents admit it, but many, I'm sure, are also embarrassed by their babies' crying and the fact that they can't console them. Establishing a routine is far from their minds.

So what can you do? Keep trying. The key to a good routine is sleep. If your baby sleeps well, he will eat well and be able to stay up for playtime. Ideally, you put a baby down before he falls asleep. At first, your difficult-to-calm baby will cry. He's used to you calming him. Don't give up. Do the same eat-play-sleep sequence over and over: feed, amuse, change, swaddle, hold, and then lay him down in the crib. If he starts crying, wait a few minutes to see if it's serious. Don't rush in if it's just a fussy "nya-nya" cry. He is just trying to settle down and doesn't yet have the skills to do it without your help. Let him try.

However, if the crying increases, you must go to him. I don't believe that babies at this age should be left to cry. (As I explain in chapter 19, when your baby is six months or older, you can use my very gentle sleep-training method that involves only a brief period of crying.) For now, pick him up. Sit in a rocking chair or on a bed with him. If he calms quickly and drifts off, put him down immediately. If he's still agitated, prop yourself up with several pillows, and keep him upright for a little while. When he stops crying and seems more relaxed, try to lay him down again. If his eyes pop open and he starts crying again, wait for a few minutes to see if he settles on his own. If necessary, go to him and start the process over.

After several rounds of this, *you* might be ready to fall asleep! And we can hope he will be, too. Put him on your chest or belly, his face turned to one side, the way he laid on you in the delivery room. Use pillows to support your arms, so that in case you doze off, your baby will be safe. (His face should not be near the pillows; they're there for *your* support.)

Start now, in the second month. Believe me, it will work if you keep at it. It doesn't matter whether you have been holding your baby constantly because he cries a lot or you've been doing it because it satisfies your need to be close to her. I've seen both. Either way, you will face huge resistance. But as I explained earlier, Mom, trying to change a bad habit later is way more difficult than if you start now. Playtime will give you plenty of opportunities to hold and cuddle her. Besides, it isn't wise to let your baby decide what's best for herself.

Eventually, especially if you start nudging her toward a routine, it will take less time to soothe your baby, and, most important, she will learn to soothe herself. Sometimes I have to persuade my clients to allow me to work on my routine and to trust that what we're doing will get the baby back on track. When, finally, they start to see that their baby is eating well, is alert and engaged, and goes to sleep with relatively few problems, they are happy and proud of their child. But, really, they should be proud of themselves.

Chapter 16

HOW ARE WE DOING?

In some households, where angelic babies live, Mom heaves a sigh of relief by the end of the second month. Although she's as sleep-deprived as any new mother, she feels more confident and relaxed in her role. In other households, where the mother has gotten off to a rough start and/or there's a difficult-to-calm baby in residence, life is chaotic. Mom is not only exhausted, but she barely has time to take a shower or plan for anything. Of course, there are a million variations in between.

Perhaps you read this book early on and have been following my advice since day one. Depending on whether your baby co-operates, you might be on track—or not. Or maybe you're a new reader, and your baby is already seven or eight weeks old. Either way, this is a good time to assess where you are. If you're one of the lucky ones, and your baby has already cut out a night feeding and is sleeping in one long stretch, keep up whatever you're doing. If not, it's too early to "train" your baby to sleep, but it's not too early to take stock. If you see at this point that certain bad habits are beginning, at least start now to undo them.

What You Can Do Now

Look at your feedings. Consider how you're feeding. If you're nursing, have you tried different positions? Are there any leftover problems that you're still dealing with? Is your baby gaining weight properly? Is he taking in increasingly larger amounts of food?

At two months, most babies should be ingesting four to six ounces of milk per feeding. If you're breast-feeding, do you see signs that your baby isn't getting enough—a hunger cry two hours after a feeding, irritability, diapers not heavily soaked? If so, pump both breasts before feeding him to check how much milk your body is producing. Then give him that expressed milk in a bottle.

Look at playtimes. By two months old, most babies can stay awake a little longer than an hour after a feeding. What's happening during playtime? Do you allow your baby any alone time? He will not learn to amuse himself unless he's allowed to spend time on his own. Have you incorporated massage into your pre-bedtime routine in place of play? Especially if you have a difficult-to-calm baby, massage can be a wonderful relaxer that helps your baby sleep.

Look at sleep. Review the steps to a good sleep routine. Do you try to put your baby to bed while he's still awake? Do you rush in quickly without waiting a few seconds to see if it's just settling-down fussiness? Have you introduced a pacifier and other good sleep associations? Do you give up easily? Do you already have books on your night table, promising to "train" your baby to sleep? Sometimes babies will take little catnaps in a bouncing chair or stroller. Is that how your baby naps *most* of the time? Do his naps tend to be less than forty-five minutes?

Look at your baby. How much of his day is spent crying? Does he have tummy troubles or a skin condition such as eczema? Does his temperament make him hard to console? How much have you been holding him? Sometimes babies need to be held. But holding to sleep should be a last resort at this age, unless your baby is having a bad day. Although he "asks" to be held by crying and needs your attention at that moment, do you continue to hold him after he's calm?

Look at yourself. What were your expectations of mother-hood? Is your baby with you all the time? Why? What are *you* getting from the experience? Can you take her crying in stride, or does it really upset you? No one likes to be in the presence of tears, but some of us have a higher threshold than others.

Regardless of your attitude and beliefs, however, some babies sleep through the night by the third month. They might wake up, but they can resettle themselves and go for a five- or six-hour stretch without your help. But those babies account for only about 10 to 20 percent of the ones I've known. At the other extreme, also about 10 to 20 percent, are difficult-to-calm babies. In between, there are many variations.

If we establish a routine from the beginning, though, even with an infant who is often uncomfortable or in pain, chances are good that he will learn to trust, despite tummy troubles or sensitivity. Even though your baby might sometimes cry more than expected, and more than you'd like, he will gradually learn how to calm himself. Little by little, he'll feel more secure. His discomfort will ease over time. He'll trust his environment (you, his close others, the household), because you have always tried to comfort and protect him. In fact, in my experience, by the third or fourth month, most difficult-to-calm babies start to have an easier time of it.

In the meantime, use every opportunity that comes along to help your baby develop self-soothing skills. Whenever your baby is calm, that's your cue. Back off, allow her to be alone and to amuse herself. Start to teach her to self-soothe. You will continue to have rough days, but at least you're moving in the right direction.

HOW DID WE GET HERE?

If you're still having a rough time in the second month, one or more of these statements about your baby or you is probably true:

+ She dozed off during feedings and got used to "snacking."
+ She suckled your breast after a feeding was over and learned to use *you* as a pacifier.
+ You didn't carve out time for play after feeding, and she goes straight from meals to bed.
+ She sleeps four or five hours at a stretch during the day and wakes frequently at night.
+ You brought her into your bed in the middle of the night.
+ You felt sorry for her, held her often, and now she relies solely on *you* for calming.
+ She was always a difficult-to-calm baby.

Notes on the Second Month

Look How Much My Baby Grew!

My baby weighs _____ pounds, which is _____ more/less than he weighed at birth.

My baby measures _____ inches, which is _____ "taller" than he was at birth.

Eat

Has your feeding routine changed? Are there any lingering problems? Do you feel more secure when you nurse or give your baby a bottle?

_____

_____

_____

_____

Play

What can your baby do now that she couldn't do a month ago? Does she stay up longer after eating? Does she have favorite toys and positions? Who are her favorite people? What does she look and sound like when she's bored? Does she enjoy her bath and massage?

_____

_____

_____

_____

Sleep

How's your baby doing on the road to Dreamland? Describe your sleep ritual, how you prepare him for naps and bedtime. How long can he last through the night without hunger or habit waking him? How long are his naps? If he's only sleeping for short spurts in the night, or only taking catnaps during the day, what are you doing to help him?

_____

_____

_____

_____

What Else Is Happening?

Here, add any other observations or thoughts about your baby's second month:

_____

_____

_____

_____

OUR ROUTINE

If you haven't already started to keep track, write down the specific times your baby eats, plays, and sleeps. If his routine is still erratic, make copies of this page and keep track for several days or more.

5: _____

6: _____

7: _____

8: _____

9: _____

10: _____

11: _____

12: _____

1: _____

2: _____

3: _____

4: _____

5: _____

6: _____

7: _____

8: _____

9: _____

10: _____

11: _____

12: _____

1: _____

2: _____

3: _____

4: _____

PHASE V

The Third Month and Beyond:
Settling In and Looking Ahead

IN A NUTSHELL

When I care for a baby from day one, I look forward to the third month, because that's when the baby becomes a little person, a true member of the family. This is a time to rejoice, because you've gotten through the hardest months. It's also another opportunity to correct course, if necessary.

COVERED IN THIS PHASE

A word to working mothers

Your growing baby: What to expect

My three-minute method

Your baby or your boss?

$\mathcal{I}$ happened to be caring for Lila, who was not quite three months old as I was writing this chapter. Her parents are both in the music business and quite successful. Many other "helpers" worked in the household during my time there, including Trisha, a very pretty and animated young woman in her early twenties. Whenever Trisha had a chance, she'd stop what she was doing to play with Lila. She'd pick her up, walk around with her, and sing songs to her. She showered Lila with kisses. Another helper, Clarice, rarely interacted with Lila. I sensed that she was either too busy or not a "baby person"—maybe both. One day, both women were in the kitchen with us. Lila was in her little chair on the table, and Clarice, the one who rarely interacted with her, said, "Hi, Lila! How are you today? Don't you look cute?" They were face-to-face, Clarice was smiling, but Lila was not. She just stared, as if she was trying to figure out who Clarice was. I said to Trisha, "See if she'll give *you* a smile." As soon as Trisha turned in her direction, Lila's eyes opened wide, and she beamed.

So, you see, Mom, baby Lila is not even three months old, and already she recognizes people who are kind to her. She already has her favorites. There is already a lot going on in her little baby mind. And in *your* baby's mind, too.

Remarkable things happen when your little one reaches the third month. Every day, she becomes more than just "the baby." You have a sense of her personality now, her likes and dislikes. And it will just keep getting better.

By the third month, if all goes well, the routine is pretty much the same. Most babies stay awake now from two to two and a half hours between feedings. Feedings will soon move from every three hours to every four (by the fifth month). Some babies at this age are able to self-soothe most of the time. Still, there are times when Mom—or Dad or whoever spends time caring for the baby—has to step in and cuddle for a bit.

As we saw in Lila's case, a three-month-old will smile at almost everyone, but her biggest smiles are reserved for people she knows best, and in most households, that's especially her mother. Just hearing Mom's familiar voice can calm her.

Your baby is older now, more social, and able to spend time alone. He can lie on a soft carpet or under a Gymini or sit slightly inclined in a baby seat, and he's content to just look around. You'll notice now that he stares at small objects, especially bright ones that stand out in his environment. You might find him gazing at a painting, for example, with a bold design or sharply contrasting colors. He's easily distracted by those red and black drawings you placed in his crib and toys that he can stare at and reach for.

You are in a new phase, too. You've gotten over many of the challenges of the earlier phases. You can bring your baby almost anywhere. You are developing a relationship with him. You can finally take a breath. The developmental leaps you'll witness over the coming months will astound you.

If you're still having a rough time getting your baby on track, it's more important than ever to continue reinforcing the eat-play-sleep routine and to continue to "school" your baby in self-soothing, especially if you're planning to go back to work. And if your baby is still having sleep issues at six months, it might be time to try my three-minute method, covered in chapter 19.

Chapter 17

A WORD TO WORKING
MOTHERS

Based on the number and variety of households I've visited, I can say with confidence that a mother who works outside the home is not a threat to her baby's happiness. Many of my clients are high-powered women who had multiple responsibilities before they became mothers. Making that transition from manager to mother meant that they had to carve out space in their busy schedules for the new role and use their time wisely.

The most successful working mothers I've met spend quality time at home in the first three months. They develop and maintain strong bonds with their babies regardless of what tugs at them from the outside. When these moms do go back to work or resume their other everyday responsibilities, they know their babies well. As working mothers, they, of course, have very busy days and nights. But despite the difficulties of dividing their time between home and work, these women become attentive, consistent, and dedicated mothers. Let's look at how they get there.

From Manager to Mother to Manager

It is an honor to watch as a woman accustomed to being in charge takes on the role of mother and allows herself to embrace the experience. The two jobs are quite different. As a manager or even just as an employee, you have experiences to draw from, realistic goals, and policies and routines in place that guide you. You can give orders. If it's a good work situation, you also have a clear idea of what it takes to be successful. But a baby is not like a project or a task you complete. For a first-time mother especially, it's like visiting another planet. Everything is new and different. Your managerial skills don't seem to matter at first, because you can't plan or predict. You just have to pay attention and learn as you go. This is often a shock to women who are used to taking charge and being in control of their time and energy.

Some adjust gracefully. These women apply who they are in the workplace to their new role. The efficient manager turns into an efficient mother, who realizes that her days now require flexibility and patience. Others struggle. They are unable or unwilling to switch gears. They spend time trying to get the baby to fit in, without first learning who he is.

Granted, some women want to work, and many more need to. My advice—assuming that you have a choice about when to return to your job—is to take the first three months off, so that you can use the time as on-the-job training for your new role as mom. If you can only take six weeks, try to go back to work part-time at first. To me, there are three keys to being a successful working mother:

1. Put in the time and energy at the beginning. During your maternity leave, learn all you can about the baby's personality and what he needs.

2. Start early to look for a reliable childcare provider, a person you will take the time to train or a facility at which you'll take the time to observe.

3. After returning to work, whenever you're at home, use your time wisely and well. Be truly *with* your baby when you're with him. By caring for him, you gain his trust. Leave your other responsibilities at the door.

If those conditions are met, your baby will soon become confident that you're still "there." He'll count on seeing you, hearing you, smelling you, and getting from you all the good sensations he's come to expect.

Believe me, Mom, the time you take now to *be* with your baby will pay off in so many ways. You will bond with her and know her. You will have the time to give her a good start, a predictable routine. There will be many days when you won't feel in control. But if you are consistent and realistic, you'll gain the confidence you need in order to leave her with another caregiver. You will know what's best for your baby. You'll know what questions to ask a prospective childcare provider. Whether you have to deal with your own mother, a nanny, or a day-care center, you'll know how to train that person to take care of your baby the way you do. Even though you'll feel pangs, you'll know that your baby will be safe and happy in your absence—and thrilled to see you when you get home.

Once you go back to work, take time to incorporate baby care into your own morning regimen. Feed and play with your baby before you leave the house. It might sadden you to leave and to know that you have to be away for the rest of the day—that's natural. Few mothers are happy about leaving their babies. But at the same time, you might be eager to get back to grown-up pursuits. That's normal, too.

When you return home, run your morning routine in reverse.

Feeding, bathing and massage, and spending quiet time to help prepare your baby to sleep will be comforting to you, too, because you'll know that you are connecting with him.

Will your baby feel your absence when you're away? Of course he will. However, your being out of the house for large portions of the day will not seem strange to him after a while. He will get used to the new routine.

And chances are, it will be hard for you, too. Especially at first, you might feel intense pangs of doubt and regret when you leave in the morning. At worst, you might overcompensate or feel guilty. But if, as I suggested in the introduction to this book, you continue to be patient, open, and attentive, I assure you that being a working mother won't compromise or break the bond between you and your new baby.

What Is Quality Time?

Quality time doesn't just happen; it depends on your attention and intention. Quality time occurs whenever you do something for or with your baby, as long as you are truly focusing on her in that moment. Cuddling together, cooing at her, dressing her, feeding her, talking to her while you go for a walk, bathing her—all of these can be moments of connection if you are truly present.

Quality time does not happen when your attention wanders. Even if you are able to multitask, resist the urge to be "efficient" when you're feeding or caring for your baby. If you're distracted— on the phone, watching TV, or having a discussion with your neighbor—you might as well let someone else feed her. I know you love your baby, but when you're with her, it's important to focus on *her* and not on your "to do" list.

Admittedly, putting in quality time as a working mother is tricky, more so if this isn't your first child. Your older ones will want your attention the minute you walk through the door. No working mother is immune. The best you can do is to know that everyone's going to want your attention and try to prepare yourself for it. Daddy can be a life saver by making more room in his schedule to care for the older children, at least for the first few months, so that you can spend most of your homecoming time with the new arrival.

The truth is, you will have to make a hundred decisions in the course of a day. What to do first? How to do it? My advice is to approach, pause, and think. Ask yourself, *Am I really paying attention? Am I doing the best for my child? Is there a better way to do this?* Babies become smarter and more alert every day. When you have to make a choice or solve a problem, ask yourself, *Will this help, or will it hurt (delay or interfere with) my child's development?*

Finding Suitable Childcare

Several months before you plan to go back to work, come up with a plan to make the transition easier for both you and your baby. Even adults are resistant to change. So why would we expect a baby to adapt immediately to a new caregiver?

Be patient. The new caregiver needs to learn what your baby is used to and, most important, what you expect. How do you know when and if a caregiver is right for your family?

The process starts with good research. Narrow down your choices. Do you want your baby cared for at home or off the premises? Only you can decide which is best. Once you've hired a person or made arrangements with a day-care facility, you enter a trial period during which you give explicit instructions to your baby's new caretaker and take time to train and observe that person.

The Research

Start early. Regardless of what kind of childcare you're planning to use—a relative, a part-time nanny, a live-in aide, a childcare facility—you'll need time to make arrangements and give the person (and your baby) a chance to get acclimated. How much lead time you'll need—a month, two, or three—depends on your situation. For example, if your mother is going to be the caretaker, she has probably already been around her grandchild and knows the ropes. Also, you know your mother! But with a stranger, you'll need time to get comfortable.

If you're considering a day-care facility, visit and watch the staff with other children. With a nanny, build in a period (at least a week or two) to train her and to observe her caring for your baby. Allow for missteps. Sometimes we think a particular person or facility is great and then realize that it is not the right choice.

Value word-of-mouth over the internet or the Yellow Pages. Visit at least three facilities, if you can find that many within a short commute. Rooms should be clean and organized, furniture free of sharp corners. Ask whether babies are segregated from older children and where they nap. Might your baby be disturbed by the sound of older children playing? The outdoor recreation areas should be clean, airy, and safe, with sunlight and shade. Toys should be in good condition, clean, and appropriate for your baby's age. If your baby is sensitive to smells and substances, ask about cleaning procedures and products.

Responsible day-care facilities give parents open access. Ask whether you can stay with your baby for the first few days or pop in for a visit while she's getting used to it. If the director says you're not allowed, look for another facility. Find out which caregivers will be attending your baby when you're not there and how many there are. Learn their names. For children less than one year old, a three-to-one ratio is ideal. As with an in-home care provider, the entire staff should be trained and certified in first aid and CPR. In addition, all emergency procedures should be clearly posted.

Gauging Fit

Interview several prospective nannies or day-care providers. The initial interview should be at least an hour long. Start with her previous experience. Has she cared for children in the same age range as your baby? Encourage her to tell you about other households and other kids with whom she has worked. In her stories, do you sense that she is patient, open, and attentive, the qualities I stress in this book? Of course, ask about safety. For example, is she trained to administer first aid and CPR? If you have a swimming pool, does she know how to swim? Does she know how to drive in case of an emergency?

Bring your baby to the interview. See how the potential nanny or day-care staff behaves toward your child and how your child reacts to them and, at a facility, to the setting itself. Ask for written references, and double-check them carefully by phone or, better still, if a former client lives in your area, in person.

Choose someone you like. Hiring a person to care for your baby is like entering into a partnership. Whether you go through a highly respected agency or you ask trusted friends for their recommendations, you need to feel both comfortable and compatible with the person and confident in his or her abilities for the relationship to work. Observe the person's personality and people skills. You'll want a calm, kind person, someone who is knowledgeable and, when necessary, can offer his or her own ideas. This person is going to be part of your household, not to mention caring for your most precious possession. The person you select must understand, respect, and follow your point of view regarding feeding, routine, discipline, and so on.

The Trial Period

Write down your routine. When I am asked to train either a new nanny or a backup person to work on a day off, the first thing I do is write down what the baby's day looks like. I don't want to leave anything to chance. Verbal instructions can be forgotten or misinterpreted. So write down everything you want a childcare provider to know about your little one's daily routine and his temperament. Include what your baby is like and how he typically reacts. What amuses him? Make a list of the songs you sing to him and the pictures he likes to look at. Does he have a cranky period? Do particular things upset him? How does he like to be comforted? All of these little bits of information will help your baby feel comfortable with someone new.

Make the transition gradually. From the first weeks of life, your baby has been able to distinguish who provides the majority of her care from others in her environment. Therefore, when your baby is cared for by a stranger and is also in an unfamiliar setting, it is important that the transition be made slowly. I spend at least a week working side-by-side with my replacement, showing how I take care of the baby. That way, I gain confidence in the person, and—even more important—I give the baby time to get to know, like, and trust her new caregiver.

Start with short time spans, a few one- or two-hour sessions. Be with the new person or at the new facility. If you're there to observe and your baby seems distressed, stepping in will ease your child's adjustment and show the caregiver what you normally do. If you have an in-home helper, try to go back to work part-time at first so that you can at least be in the background while your baby and the new person are getting to know each other. Make yourself available, but don't hover. If you have someone who's had a lot of experience, you might also learn from the nanny.

Leave a list of emergency phone numbers. This list should

include your number, Dad's, the pediatrician's, and those of trustworthy individuals who are willing to step in if you can't be reached. Be clear about what to do—for example, when to call 911 and whom to call first. Give the person your health insurance information. Find out whether emergency facilities in your locale require a letter or power-of-attorney before allowing a caregiver to act on your behalf. It's also a good idea to have the new caregiver come to your baby's next checkup to meet your pediatrician and get acquainted with the staff.

Expect a period of adjustment. Babies are very vulnerable, so of course, your first concern is your child's welfare. Make sure that he is kept on his usual feeding, playing, and sleeping routine. At the same time, though, know that your baby might be harder for a stranger to handle. The new caregiver can't "read" him as well as you do. Your baby will also sense the difference and perhaps be more on edge than usual. Even if you've found someone who has great compassion and a lot of patience, it will take time.

Every day, when you come home from work, ask questions and observe your baby. By now, you know your child. If you notice that your baby is suddenly having trouble settling down at night or is eating differently, perhaps the caregiver isn't keeping him on the routine you laid out. Rather than accuse, though, ask good questions. Ideally, you've hired someone honest and open, and you've let the person know you always want to hear the truth. Otherwise, there is no point in asking anything!

Any reputable person or day-care center won't mind your asking questions: How was his day? How long did he sleep? Did he go down easily? Did he poop? What did you two do today? What toys did he play with? Did he spend time on his tummy? Did you go for a walk? The point is not to interrogate the nanny or day-care staff. Instead, have a friendly conversation, be open, and ask lots of questions about how the day went. Encourage the care provider to ask questions, too.

Have reasonable expectations for your caregiver. When I train a nanny to take over, I explain everything so that there are no surprises. Some of my clients expect their childcare providers to do housework, in addition to taking care of the baby. They figure that the baby naps at least a few hours during the day, so they ask the nanny to do "a few extras"—dishwashing, cooking, vacuuming, laundry (for everyone, not just the baby's). It's best to state your expectations before the person is hired. Unfortunately, that's not always how it goes. Some nannies I know refuse jobs that involve housework, and they're likely to quit when asked to do chores that weren't previously discussed.

If you expect the person who takes care of your child to do other tasks, do those tasks yourself, at least once. Time how long each job takes, and ask yourself, *Where is my baby going to be while the person is busy?* In other words, be sure that you're making reasonable demands on the caregiver's time, because that person's priority should be the baby, not housework.

Be honest with your child. Never try to "sneak out" on your baby. He will learn not to trust you and is likely to become hypervigilant whenever you're with him, because he's afraid that you'll disappear again without warning. Tell him that you're leaving, and use the same phrase over and over, something simple, such as "I'll be back soon." Even if he cries when you leave, each time you come back, he'll trust you a little bit more.

And if you're tempted to think, *She's just a baby—she won't know the difference*, remember how little Lila preferred one household helper over another. She wasn't even three months old, and she knew a lot about her environment and the people in it. Never assume that your child doesn't get it. Even if she can't talk, even if her brain is not actually capable of deep thinking, she *feels*. She knows what's familiar and comfortable—and by paying attention, so will you.

WHAT IF . . . **I'm Not Happy with the Caretaker I've Hired?**

Although planning, careful research, and explicit instructions usually lead to a good caretaking solution, sometimes a nanny or a day-care facility doesn't work out.

Try to figure out why. You can only take steps to better a bad situation if you understand the reasons. It could be any (or more than one) of the following or an issue that is specific to your situation:

- The caretaker is not following your routine or your instructions.

- The caretaker has other children to watch and is not giving yours proper attention.

- The caretaker is spending too much time on personal tasks, such as talking on the phone.

- You and the caretaker disagree frequently or lock horns.

- There is friction between the caretaker and other members of your household.

Ask yourself, *Have I taken the time to observe and give guidance?* No one knows your baby as well as you do. In order to feel comfortable yourself and for another person to do the job well, you have to give good information.

Talk honestly about your concerns. Be specific ("I notice that Frederico is always cranky when I come home"). Give the caretaker a chance to explain ("Why do you think that's happening?"). Try not to accuse. Instead, get as much information as you can ("Why don't you and I run through the day, so I can understand what happens when I'm not here").

Unless there's been a serious breach of trust or your baby is in danger, consider giving the person a second chance. After you've clarified the problem, let the person know that you'll give it another week (or two, depending on what you're comfortable with). During that time, ask the person to keep a log of what happens while you're away. Drop in unannounced. Notice changes in your baby.

Don't act hastily or impulsively. Before you fire the nanny or take your baby out of the day-care facility, know what your options are. If you decide to go another route, you will have to take the time to start the whole process from the beginning—the research, the interviews, the trial period.

Chapter 18

YOUR GROWING BABY:
WHAT TO EXPECT

In this chapter, I look at what you can expect past the three-month mark and what kinds of new challenges you might face. This chapter will help you understand how miraculously and quickly your baby will change. Looking ahead, paying attention, and being aware of these changes in the coming months will help you help your baby. For each age range below, I describe what to expect and also look at possible issues that might come up at that point or in the coming months.

You'll notice that there are no "What If . . ." features in this chapter. That's because babies' development varies widely. Some babies, for example, sit up at seven months, others at nine. If you suspect that your baby is not on track, talk to your pediatrician. But also remember that there's a wide range of "normal" during the first year.

The Fourth and Fifth Months

These two months are quite similar. Your baby is engaging more. His eyes follow you around the room. You can talk to him when he's crying, and he's starting to understand. "Hi, little one, is that a reason to cry? Be happy . . . Mommy is here, and you are OK." He is able to distract himself by looking at his hands, sucking his fingers, or just looking around. He smiles at familiar faces. He also might cry when face-to-face with someone he doesn't recognize. Family and friends who visit infrequently might be offended. Suggest nicely that they give him a chance to get used to them.

Older babies are able to ingest more milk and last longer, so feedings can go from three to four hours apart. Some babies start to wean themselves from the nighttime feeding as early as the third or fourth month, which is fine as long as they weigh at least fourteen pounds and have five or six six-ounce bottles during the day, taking in approximately thirty ounces of milk per twenty-four hours. Whether they're breast-fed or formula-fed, babies eat the same amount by now.

Your baby's body is getting prepared for solid food, too, which typically happens around six months. Large babies can start as early as four or five months. Your pediatrician will determine if your baby needs solid food before six months. However, as with all developmental milestones, the timing—determined largely by heredity—differs from child to child.

Because your baby is eating more efficiently, she spends less time draining a breast or bottle, allowing her a longer playtime, which is now more like real play. Give your baby toys that she can hold and put in her mouth. She will appreciate anything that makes a noise. You can also play simple games, such as peek-a-boo. If you haven't already started, make reading one of her daily activities. At this age, just show her the pictures, and make up your own words and stories. If you pay attention, you'll see that she has a favorite book, because she'll get excited when she sees it. She's "telling" you to show her more. Undoubtedly, you've already begun to take her for long walks. If not, start, because both of you will enjoy them.

By now, your baby should be comfortable in a variety of positions. On his back, he will try to reach for the toys hanging from his mobile or Gymini. If you followed my advice and gave him tummy time in the first month, you'll now see why. He's comfortable in the prone position, which will help him learn to crawl. During the next few months, he'll realize he can inch along the floor and "swim," flailing his arms and legs while lying on his belly. Then he'll get up on his knees, which means he's getting ready to crawl.

You can also work on a new position: sitting. Sit on the floor, and put her between your legs, so that your body supports her back and keeps her body centered. Eventually, she'll be able to sit there by herself.

Possible Fourth- and Fifth-Month Issues

Teething. Your baby might start to teethe now. His baby teeth pushing through the gums will be painful at times and also cause him to drool, so be sure to have plenty of bibs on hand. Sometimes a baby drools so much that his entire chest can get wet. Also, since his gums are sore, he'll act like a puppy, chewing on anything he can get his hands on. That's why rattles and soft toys are good for babies at this age. Generally, the two front bottom teeth come in first. Later, the upper front teeth break through, followed by the bottom incisors, the first molars, and, last, the canines.

The pressure of the teeth pushing against the baby's gums can be painful, especially when he's lying down. Even when he's upright, he might be bothered by a tingling in his gums, a sensation that some babies find irritating. No surprise, then, that teething (during the next few months) might interfere with your routine. When those little teeth cut through your baby's gums, it can disrupt his sleep. Signs of teething include being more irritable than usual, pulling on his ears, or running a slight fever. Ask your pediatrician's opinion about alleviating the discomfort. Don't be surprised if, after several nights in a row of your holding him to sleep, your baby has trouble sleeping without your help, even if he was a good sleeper before. Be consistent with your sleep ritual. Give him his sleep aids, put him in the crib while he's still awake, and if he doesn't settle after a few "nya-nya" cries, comfort him and try again.

Early waking. Many babies give up the middle-of-the-night feeding around four or five months and then start to wake up earlier. Again, I urge you to wait before rushing in, so as to discourage this early-bird pattern. The problem is, she might be hungry—her last feeding was six or eight hours ago—and probably can't hold her own bottle yet. (Most babies don't do this until around six or seven months.) If she keeps crying, she's hungry. Feed her as if it's nighttime (without conversation), and then put her down in her crib. She might fall back to sleep.

If she doesn't fall back to sleep, encourage her at least to play in her crib. She might cry when you leave the room, especially if you haven't already started giving her some "alone time." Still, keep trying. If you give her the opportunity, she'll learn to go back to sleep and awaken again at a more reasonable time, say somewhere between seven and eight A.M. I understand that by the time you're done with the feeding, it will be close to six. But ignore that. Unless you have to rush her to day care right away, it is still too early for her to get up. And don't bring her into your bed. You'll thank me later!

Illness. Your baby might be vulnerable to colds now. If you stopped breast-feeding, he has to rely on his own immune system, which isn't yet fully developed. Also, he visits a wider variety of public places. If there are older siblings in your household, they bring home germs, too. I've seen babies with siblings catch a cold and spend the better part of their first year with a runny nose.

However, sneezes and a stuffy nose aren't always signs of a cold. Because a baby has such a small air passage, lingering portions of mucus, very dry air, cigarette smoke, or other airborne substances can cause symptoms that mimic a cold. Whatever the cause of your baby's discomfort—cold, allergies, intestinal flu—do everything you can to comfort her, but once she's on the road to recovery, get right back to the routine.

The Sixth Month

Your baby is making great physical strides by now. He sits up better, rolls over, and probably prefers to sleep on his tummy. This is a time we can relax and let babies sleep in whatever position they find comfortable. But we also have to keep the crib free of blankets and look for other ways he might get into trouble. Remember, your baby is now spending a lot of time alone in his crib.

When you shop for toys, select playthings that are educational and age-appropriate (look on the package) and that inspire your baby to have fun and to develop her senses. Babies this age love noise toys and musical gadgets, but use your common sense. Don't overwhelm your baby with too much stimulation.

The floor is the best play area, because it gives her a wide-angle view, engages her curiosity, and motivates her to reach and "scooch"—do the G.I. Joe army crawl—toward interesting objects in the room. Try to vary the play from exciting to quiet activities. I always keep a basket of picture books within reach for winding down. Your baby probably already has her favorites.

By far, your baby's best "toy" is another human. She loves to play silly games with everyone, especially older siblings.

The most exciting event of your baby's sixth month is solid food. Adding cereal, fruits and vegetables and, later, other foods, will change his feeding routine. To start, you will introduce solids once a day. For the next several months, even as you add various new foods to his diet, his main source of protein will continue to be breast milk or formula. However, at around a year, he'll have three meals a day and snacks in between.

Possible Sixth-Month Issues

Too-short naps. At six months, some babies are good nappers, especially if they've been on a consistent routine, and others are not. Babies needs their naps now more than ever, because their days are filled with activity. Ideally, your baby now has two naps during the day. I prefer a short morning nap and then a longer one—at least an hour and a half, if not two hours long—after lunch, around one P.M. Of course, it depends on the baby and his particular sleep history.

Some mothers are still grappling with a too-short nap pattern that started four months ago. If instead of having at least one solid nap a day, your baby is still in the habit of catnapping, sleeping forty-five minutes or less, teething can make it worse. The extra saliva and, sometimes, the pain wake babies up. But the bigger culprit, as I mentioned earlier, is that once babies become portable, they prefer to sleep in their carriages or car seats. If your baby wakes up cranky after a too-short nap, she is probably tired, which affects how she eats and plays. You need to help her. Assuming that your baby is starting solid food and weighs at least fourteen pounds, you can use my three-minute method (see chapter 19).

Allergic reactions. If your baby has very sensitive skin, certain foods can give her a rash. As a precaution, instead of trying to wipe off the food with a napkin or a dry cloth, I use a warm, wet washcloth, no soap. Too much rubbing can irritate her delicate skin. When I'm at the park and don't have access to water, I use an unscented, premoistened wipe.

Confusion about solid foods. Below, I try to help you understand how and when to introduce solid foods. It can be tricky. Eating solids is harder to gauge than your baby's liquid intake. You might wonder, *Is my baby eating enough? Should milk be continued in the same proportions?* The risk is that you might offer your baby more food than she needs or, even worse, try to force her to eat even when she is satisfied. I never force a healthy baby to eat.

Some Advice About Solid Foods

Even if no allergies run in your family, it's really important to introduce solid food carefully, holding off on certain harder-to-digest foods (see below). Here is the plan I follow:

> First, integrate solid foods and new liquids into your feeding routine. Some mothers buy prepared baby foods; others like to puree their own, which requires extra planning, time, and effort. Once you cook and puree the food, you can freeze it in small portions, for example, in an ice tray.

> Continue giving your baby breast milk or formula. It will be the mainstay of her diet until she is a year old. After feeding liquids, wait an hour and a half to two hours to feed your baby solids. Otherwise, she might be too full. For example, you might give her a breast or a bottle at 11 and solids at 1. After she is fed and washed up, she can have a little playtime. Then give her a bottle, and she's ready for her afternoon nap. Whereas I didn't advise breast-feeding or

giving a bottle to sleep when your baby was younger, now that she's six months or older, there's no risk of getting her into a bad habit, so she can have a bottle to help her relax before naps and bedtime.

› Get your child used to drinking water. I assure you, he will like it. Juices have a lot of sugar, so I give my babies actual fruits. Even when your baby gets older, fruit juice shouldn't be an everyday drink. And I don't give children soda—at any age!

› Feed her in a high chair. Most have two or three positions. Depending on how well your baby sits up—most don't at six months—keep the chair back in an inclined position, so it doesn't put too much strain on her back. Use a bib; at first, feedings are messy. To encourage your baby to open her mouth, give her a spoon. I'm not suggesting that she's ready to feed herself. But when she holds anything, I'm sure you'll notice that she automatically brings it to her mouth. This simple strategy will make it easier to feed her. When I start to feed a baby in a high chair, I put a toy on the tray for her to play with while I prepare the food. But once she starts to eat, I only give a spoon or two. I don't believe that children should get used to playing while eating. No TV, either. We eat with our eyes and with our mouths.

› Start with cereal. Cereal—rice or oatmeal specially formulated for babies—is an ideal starter food, given once a day at first, usually at breakfast, approximately an hour after her morning bottle. If it's more convenient, you can also do this once-a-day meal at lunchtime. Mix two teaspoons of cereal with breast milk or formula. The mushy consistency

will help your baby get used to ingesting something denser.
Mixing cereal with a liquid that's already familiar also
makes it easier for him to adapt to the taste. By the way,
Mom, always taste what you give your baby. If a food tastes
bad to you, your baby probably won't like it, either.

› Introduce light-colored fruits and vegetables first. Start
with fruit. After three days of cereal, smash a ripe banana,
and add it to the cereal. Gradually move on to other light-
colored fruits, such apples and pears. Give her one or more
fruits (puréed at first, later when she starts finger foods,
in small pieces) in the morning, preferably after the first
breast- or bottle-feeding.

› Next, introduce puréed vegetables, such as carrots and
sweet potatoes, which most babies instantly love. As your
baby gets older and more accustomed to solids, add new
fruits and green vegetables, and eventually, she'll eat a wide
variety of foods.

› Give one new food at a time. For instance, don't offer
peaches for the first time on the same day you introduce
apples. Once you give your baby a small amount (one
teaspoon) of a new food, wait at least four days until
you try another one. Look for changes in her mood, her
comfort level, or her skin. After a month of trial and error,
your baby will probably be ready to have two solid meals
a day—breakfast and lunch—but her main nutrition will
continue to be milk.

› Start adding a second meal of solids about two weeks later.
After about a month or two, the baby is eating two or three
puréed vegetables at lunch.

INTRODUCING HARDER-TO-DIGEST FOODS

Some foods require more caution than others. Your pediatrician can help guide you by taking into consideration your baby's weight and growth and your family history, in order to analyze whether your baby is at risk for allergies. The following are generally accepted guidelines for gradually introducing harder-to-digest foods. Your pediatrician might advise you to hold off on some of these for a few extra months.

- At seven months: egg yolks
- At eight months: meats
- At nine months: soy products, such as tofu, beans, yogurt, and cheese
- At twelve months: cow's milk, egg whites, fish, chestnuts, chocolate, citrus fruits, tomatoes and strawberries, and any foods prepared with those ingredients, such as breads and biscuits. Also, wait a year before giving honey to your little one; it contains spores that can be harmful to younger babies.

Watching a baby taste new foods will be one of your greatest delights. Don't rush the process. As your little one becomes accustomed to solids, sometime around the seventh month, add "dinner." After the eighth month, I add meats. For dessert, babies love a nice fruit puree. At one year, you can mix yogurt with the fruit.

The Seventh Month

As early as three or four months, your baby began to recognize people in her daily life—parents, caretakers, siblings. Earlier, though, she had to *see* an object (or person) to remember that it existed. At seven months, out of sight is no longer out of mind, thanks to her developing brain. Even though a familiar object, such as Mommy, is not visible to her, she can keep you in her mind. She can recognize grandparents and others who visit the household from time to time. She will also begin to prefer some over others.

Possible Seventh-Month Issues

Night feeding. Once your baby is on at least some solid foods and getting ample nutrition during the day, he shouldn't be getting night feedings or getting you up at night. If he is, you'll find solutions in chapter 19.

Separation anxiety. Sometime around the seventh month (or later), you also might have to deal with your baby's separation anxiety. He might be more reluctant to go to others in the household and wary around strangers. He might protest, as he's never done, when you leave the room during the day or when you put him down for a nap or at bedtime. If he's been having sleep issues all along, then his need for you will seem more urgent. But even babies who have been on a good routine and who know how to soothe themselves can get upset at this age when separated from their mothers.

Dealing with separation anxiety will require a little more patience, awareness, and effort on your part. Talk to your baby when you leave the room. Depart with a cheery "Be right back." The good news is that the more you reinforce this ritual of going and coming, the sooner he will begin to realize that you come back.

The Eighth Month

Researchers refer to eight-month and older babies as "little scientists." They're always exploring. Your baby wants to touch everything—and then put it in her mouth! Every waking minute, she's learning about the world around her.

Mmmmm, her little brain wonders as she notices that her father's shoe is within reach. *What does this taste like?* Sitting in her high chair, she will smash her food, pour water or juice into her plate, and look up curiously to see what unfolds. *What happens if I drop this piece of cheese onto the floor?* And so she learns, for example, that a falling object goes down, not up.

She can sit and soon will try to stand. She has the strength to get herself across the room and the manual dexterity to pick things up. Some babies also start to crawl now; some never crawl. It depends on genes and how much tummy time they've had.

If you haven't already started, give your baby bite-sized finger foods, a first step toward feeding herself. Anything that will easily dissolve in your baby's mouth can become a finger food. At first, she'll use her hands. But in a few months, as her motor coordination improves, she'll want to try a spoon. Your job is to help her learn how.

Your little scientist needs a safe play area for her experiments. When she starts to walk (a few do as early as eight or nine months), she will support herself on the furniture and try to make her way around the room, touching every object she encounters. You might come into the bathroom one day to discover that she's unrolled the toilet paper. It's not too early to start saying "No!"

Babies in my care have freedom to explore safely. But there are certain things, even at this young age, that I limit or avoid. For example, if the baby keeps throwing his food on the floor, it's not an accident. He's invented a "game." That's very bright of him. But food is to eat, not to play with. I correct by saying no, and I take the plate away. It's OK to start discipline now (see chapter 20).

Possible Eighth-Month Issues

Safety around the house. Your baby can be a danger to herself. To avoid accidents, imagine your home from her perspective. Get on the floor; look at the room from her level to see what kinds of objects spell danger—for example, electrical outlets, cords, lamps, and (assuming your house still has landlines) phone wires. Place childproof catches on cupboard doors and drawers. Move electronics, valuables, and breakable objects out of reach. Cover electrical outlets with plastic covers. No matter how good you are at "baby-proofing," though, you must constantly watch your baby, because it will be a while before she understands the concept of danger.

Create safe areas where your almost-toddler can be curious without painful consequences. For example, you open and close doors and drawers. Your baby will want to imitate you. So leave one or two cupboard doors unlocked, and use those spaces for storing plastic containers or toys. Even the simple act of opening and closing a cabinet will help his cognitive and physical development.

Eating hazards. Your child is very busy now; she can do other things while eating, such as banging a toy on her high-chair tray, but she shouldn't. It's best for her to concentrate. Encourage her to chew, not talk, while eating—both to teach her manners and to keep her safe. Even if she's just babbling, "Ma, ma, ma," food can go down the wrong "pipe." Don't make her laugh while she's eating—or attempt to discipline her. If she starts to cry with food in her mouth, she could choke. Finally, never give her food while she's walking or running.

She's having more big-girl food now and starting to feed herself finger foods, which is another potential danger. Don't allow her to feed herself without adult supervision, even when a food is considered safe. Raw vegetables and fruits are certainly healthy but hard to chew and easy to choke on. Until she has molars designed to grind what she puts in her mouth, cut finger foods into shapes that aren't round; for example, give her cubes of tender meat or cheese, and cut grapes into quarters. Take the skin off an apple before cutting it into bite-sized pieces (approximately the size of a Cheerio). Stay away from other hard fruits and from candy, peanuts, hot dogs, and popcorn. Eventually, she can start to eat what and when the rest of the family eats.

The Ninth Month and Beyond

Now your baby is exhibiting astounding physical, mental, and even emotional growth. She might be walking and/or talking and is more socially at ease. She doesn't really play *with* other babies, but she's fascinated by them. Her mind is zipping along, ever the little scientist, taking it all in. In the best situations, the early challenges of motherhood are a distant memory. At parties, you probably joke about those sleepless nights. Your baby eats and sleeps well, and you get through the day with the usual ups and downs of living with a toddler.

Possible Issues of the Ninth Month and Beyond

Strangers and new situations. If you have been your child's mainstay until now, or even if she's been with a nanny or at a day-care center, she now might feel anxious when you're not around. She probably has a favorite toy or security blanket—or both—which will help make her time away from you a little easier. But all her senses are engaged, and she's getting smarter every day. She's much more aware of her surroundings and understands way more conversation than she did six months ago. She has developed a strong attachment to you. Create a "good-bye" ritual that lets her know you're going. Use phrases such as "I'll be right back" or "Mommy has to go to work now." Give her a kiss on each cheek. Wave bye-bye.

Lingering problems with sleep. Once a baby is nine months old, he turns an important developmental corner. Bad sleep patterns are not as easily changed. Not only do babies cry at bedtime, but those who do often cry a lot. Among the most common scenarios:

> ˃ It's an ordeal to get him to sleep at night.

> ˃ He's clingy and dependent on you to soothe him.

> ˃ He's still waking up for a feeding at night.

In the next chapter, I give you some tools that will help.

Chapter 19

MY THREE-MINUTE METHOD

After working with so many parents, I have found that some just can't bear to hear their babies cry. But there comes a point in most households where parents finally have to do *something* that will help get their babies back on track. Ideally, they don't wait as long as the Russells, whose story I share in this chapter.

Helen and Warren Russell are a high-profile couple. You met their son, Oliver, in chapter 10. Both parents are professionals, very smart and powerful. We met when Helen, age thirty-eight, was in her sixth month of pregnancy. This was going to be her first child and Warren's fourth. He was close to sixty and had three adult children from a previous marriage.

One of the first things most prospective clients ask when they're deciding whether to hire me is "Do you believe in letting a baby cry?" I always say no. If a baby is in need of comfort, feeding, or changing or if he has discomfort or pain, then I believe we must help. When the topic came up with the Russells, Warren said, "I don't believe in crying."

The Cry-It-Out Questions

Most parents don't want their babies to cry. They also love the idea of getting their children to sleep throughout the night, but, like Warren, they're often not willing to let their babies cry in order to achieve it.

I always give my opinion to parents, but I never go against their wishes. No matter how much experience I have, this is *their* baby. In the Russells' case, the baby wasn't even born when the conversation about crying first came up. So I just listened. I knew that in six months, if we had to help their baby go to sleep or change a bad habit, I could help Mom and Dad see that they might have to tolerate at least a little crying.

In an adult's mind, crying means sadness, pain, discomfort, despair, loneliness. Whatever natural protective instincts we have toward infants, when we listen to a crying baby, we want to do something. Holding, bouncing, or rocking seems harmless enough. Besides, watching your child drift off to dreamland, feeling the weight of his body, is more than just a pleasant experience for a parent. It feels magical.

But months later, it often doesn't feel quite so magical. It certainly doesn't feel magical when you and your husband can't get through dinner without interruption. And there's nothing magical about being woken by a crying baby in the middle of the night or, worse, several times a night. The baby is bigger, you're sleep-deprived, and you might also have to get up for work the next morning. You put him down. But thirty minutes later, he wakes up and starts to move around until he is fully awake—and guess what? He calls you in his "language": "UWAH! UWAH! UWAH!" When he cries, he's "asking" you to hold him. You'll do anything it takes to get him to sleep again.

At this point, even parents who "don't believe in crying" start looking for an alternative. When I say it's time to "train" the baby to sleep, they usually ask three questions.

Why must a baby learn to go to sleep on his own? Both of you need your sleep. And when a pattern like I've described above becomes too deeply etched in your baby's brain, each time he wakes and can't fall back to sleep he will expect you to intervene. At some point, we have to change that pattern and change his expectations.

How can constant holding be bad for a baby? If you hold your baby all the time, you reinforce the way he learned to sleep when he was nesting inside you. Let me explain. The typical mother-to-be is active during pregnancy. She goes to work, drives, walks, works out. She wonders why her unborn child is so "quiet" during the day and is amazed that he starts moving most at night when she's lying in bed. That's because her daytime activity feels like rocking and puts him to sleep. At night, when the movement stops, he wakes up—and stays up. The next morning, the mom-to-be says, "That baby kicked all night." The baby arrives a few months later. And when Mom goes to bed, her newborn wakes up. It's what he's used to. If his mother now continues to rock him constantly or carry him around all day, she is reinforcing the pattern.

What do you mean by "at least some crying"? If we follow a routine from the beginning, give the baby cuddling during playtime and only when he needs comforting, chances are that we will not need to tolerate any hard crying. All the strategies I've written about so far are designed to meet your baby's needs, get him into a routine, and gently train him to self-soothe without much crying, or at least with a minimum of crying. I give him little opportunities to calm himself, by putting him into the crib awake, waiting to see if he can go to sleep on his own, and never rushing in when he first wakes up.

With young babies, when a fussy cry turns into something

more serious, I comfort immediately and then repeat the same pattern, as many times as necessary. Given this kind of early attention and nurturing, most babies gradually become better at self-soothing. However, if by the sixth month, a baby has trouble falling asleep, wakes frequently at night, and hasn't learned how to put himself back to sleep, it's time to give him a little push. But it has to be a *little* push. I never let my babies cry longer than three minutes.

You might wonder how I came up with three minutes. Based on my experience with babies, three minutes is a good limit to set when it comes to crying. It's also something that most moms and dads can tolerate. For the baby, the method eventually breaks the pattern, because it gives him three-minute practice sessions in self-soothing.

WHAT IF . . . I Can't Tolerate Even a Minute of Crying?

Honestly, I have no answer for you. Babies cry; it's how they express themselves. A baby also cries when she's used to a certain pattern and you try to change it. She feels uncomfortable and complains by crying.

Sleep training always involves some tears, but consider the alternative. From what I've seen, parents who can't sleep-train their babies end up with a "family bed." They might not call it that, and if you ask them whether they believe in the philosophy, they often say they don't. These parents usually just give up, because taking the baby into their bed is easier than rocking her to sleep every hour. They do it not because they're taking charge, but because they feel helpless.

Before You Even Try to Sleep-Train Your Baby

Typically, when I'm asked to "sleep-train" a baby, here are the three most common scenarios:

› The baby doesn't need the extra nutrition but still wakes in the middle of the night.

› The baby can't settle into sleep. He only falls asleep in Mom's arms or something else that rocks, such as a car seat. He wakes up the moment he's placed in his crib.

› The baby has gotten used to sleeping for only a short period of time (both at night and during naps).

What all three situations have in common is a baby who hasn't learned to soothe himself. It might be because of the baby's temperament or because of illness or other complications early on. Mom has been spending a lot of the day nursing, rocking, and holding. At play groups with other moms, she's the one who complains most about motherhood and thinks it's so "hard." One exhausted mother I met decided never to have another child.

If that sounds familiar, and your baby is six months or older, weighs at least fourteen pounds, and has no other health issues, it's probably time to take action.

It's also important to ask yourself, *Am I ready to sleep-train my baby?* In all my years of working with parents and babies, I've learned never to suggest a method that the parents don't feel comfortable doing. Regardless of how much your friends rave or how strongly a book recommends a particular approach, if it doesn't sound right and you're not ready, do not do it. You have to feel at ease, sure that you're not "hurting" your baby.

Mothers often wonder how they will know whether the baby's cry is something they have to respond to. Of course, if your baby is hungry, you have to feed her. If she's in pain, you have to comfort her. If it's any kind of emergency, you must respond right away. But if she is crying because she's used to having you there, that's another story. By six months, she's already learning to turn to her pacifier and other security items for comfort. These tools will help her get back to sleep on her own, but you have to give her the opportunity to use them. That's what those three minutes are for.

If you decide to move ahead, it's also important that your husband or partner agrees about sleep training and is willing to participate and support the effort. If not—and I've seen this happen—one parent stands there with a stopwatch, timing the baby's cry. She's made her decision and is at peace with it. Then the baby cries, and Dad rushes past her into the nursery. As he picks up the baby, Dad glares at Mom as if to say, "How could you be so cruel?" It also could be that Mom caves in and accuses Dad of being heartless. Either way, you can't let that happen. Have an ongoing discussion until you agree on a plan. Sleep training rarely works if one of you isn't on board.

Ending Night Waking: Oliver's Story

And that brings us back to the Russell household. Remember that Oliver's dad didn't "believe in" his baby crying. Let me share with you what happened once I got the job.

I started my usual routine, letting Oliver lead the way the first week or so, and then we repeated the eat-play-sleep pattern every day.

Aside from a shaky beginning because Helen's breast milk came in slowly, Oliver nursed well. He usually woke up a few times in the middle of the night but went back to sleep easily once he was fed. In the morning he got up around six, but because Helen and I had agreed that his day would start around seven or seven thirty, I didn't go to him immediately. Most of the time, he would fall asleep again. Oliver took two naps every day, one in the morning around nine thirty and a longer one around one P.M. He was also great at bedtime, settling down most evenings without any problem. Having a stable routine helped: feeding, bathing, massage. Then I'd feed him again, swaddle him, give him a pacifier and his soft, floppy white lamb, and put him into his crib. When he was about three months old, we included a story in our bedtime ritual.

For the first ten to twelve weeks, I had to go to Oliver a few times after putting him down, because he'd cry. But I always tried to calm him in his crib. I'd just give him his pacifier and gently pat his back. I would go back as many times as needed and do the exact same thing. Only if his crying intensified would I take him out of his bed. I'd then comfort him for a few seconds and, when he stopped crying, immediately lay him down again.

A lot of work? Yes, but I knew the hard work would pay off down the road and that Oliver would eventually not need my help to fall asleep. Sure enough, by four months, he knew what to expect and was happy to get into his crib even when he did not fall asleep right way.

But that's not the end of the story. Oliver was still feeding in the middle of the night at ten months. In other households, around the six-month mark, if a baby is eating liquids and solids, I start to wean him from that nighttime feeding. But in Oliver's case, his father's "no crying" rule interfered. I kept giving him that middle-of-the-night feeding to avoid any crying.

In my work, I sometimes have to take the long road, because my client is in charge. As early as the fifth month, I suspected that Oliver was no longer hungry during the night. He woke up because he was used to being fed, and it comforted him. I knew it was time for him to learn to skip the three A.M. feeding and soothe himself back to sleep. But I also respected Warren's wishes.

Did continuing those nighttime feedings hurt Oliver? Not at all. He wasn't overweight, and one extra feeding wasn't going to make him chubby. However, it trained him to expect the comfort and the nutrients, too. At some point, we would have to reverse that training.

As it happened, when Oliver was almost ten months old, I took another job but promised to stay long enough to work with a new nanny. It didn't seem as if Oliver was going to give up the night feeding without intervention. Some babies do, but by ten months, it's less likely. If we waited, it would only become harder to wean Oliver from the night feedings and get him to sleep through on his own.

I approached Helen first. "I think it would be better if you allowed me to wean Oliver off his three A.M. feeding . . . before a new nanny is hired. It's going to mean some crying. But I know that Oliver will be more responsive to me than to a stranger. He's used to my style, and he trusts me." I knew from experience that in challenging times, a baby is calmer when attended by someone with whom he has developed a bond.

Helen didn't need much convincing, and to my surprise, neither did Warren. By then, he trusted me, too. Everything else I'd done for Oliver so far—helping him to gain weight, teaching him how to self-soothe—was paying off. His little boy went to sleep easily and on his own at bedtime.

Besides, those middle-of-the-night feedings made life harder for all of the Russells, even though it was my job to tend to the baby. Helen and Warren didn't have to get out of bed, but they slept with a baby monitor in their room, so they heard everything, and it often interrupted their sleep, too. Helen had gone back to work as a movie producer, and on the days she had to supervise shoots, she left for work when it was still dark. Warren, a well-known patent attorney, also kept long hours. Oliver's night life exhausted them.

How My Three-Minute Method Works

So how do we help a baby become a good sleeper? In the beginning, it seems that you will never get there. But I promise, you eventually will. Little by little!

Start with the basic sleep ritual, which is the same for all babies: feed, bathe and massage, darken the room, place the baby in his crib (with sleep aids) while he's still awake. If your baby cooperates, great. If not, you need to do more, as follows.

Break the crying cycle. If you know that your baby isn't hungry or in pain, let her cry for three minutes. If that's too long, wait as long as you can stand it. Now, this is the tricky part. As you wait out those three minutes, which will seem like a very long time at first, you will have mixed feelings. Part of you will know you're doing the right thing. She's crying because she's used to your holding or feeding her to sleep, and you want to help her break that pattern. But another part of you might worry. *What if something's wrong? What if my baby needs something? What if this is an emergency?*

If you are not able to judge the cry, go into her room before the three minutes are up. See what the problem is. Next time, you will know better whether she's in trouble or not. The more you practice this strategy, the better you'll be at knowing whether a cry needs your attention or it's OK to sit tight for three minutes.

Some people believe that by going in after three minutes, you're teaching your baby to cry for three minutes (or whatever time you pick). I don't believe that's true. Babies do not have an understanding of time the way we do. What they will learn, if no one immediately comes in to soothe them, is how to soothe themselves.

When you go back to her room, don't stimulate her. Remember my nighttime rule: no talking, no fussing over her. Night care should be uninteresting and unstimulating. Otherwise, she might think it's playtime. Keep the room in total darkness or, if you can't see well enough, at least very dim. I repeat: Don't talk to her. First, try to calm her *in the crib*. Then give her the pacifier and/or her security object and leave the room.

Stand outside the door to her room. One three-minute period might be enough for your baby. She might fuss a little and then put herself to sleep. Or she might cry for three minutes straight, in which case, you start the process again.

Go in again—and again—if necessary. If your baby continues to cry after being comforted, wait another three minutes. Go back into her room, without turning on the lights. Again, try to soothe her without holding her. If she uses a pacifier, sucking on it will usually do the trick. Pick her up if she starts screaming. If you have to hold her for a few minutes to calm her, don't wait until she falls asleep. Put her back into the crib while she's still awake. When you put her down and leave the room, she might protest. Wait another three minutes before you go back in.

How many times you go back into the room depends on the baby. Some give up crying by the second or third time. They suck on their pacifiers or gaze at their mobiles, and they eventually fall asleep. Your waiting teaches your baby that there's another way to go to sleep, one that doesn't involve an adult. Other babies take longer to learn. Still, this is a gentle process. It doesn't allow your baby to cry too hard or for too long, because you always comfort her after three minutes. Those babies who have never learned how to sleep without being rocked require lots of patience. If you have to go back more than two or three times, chances are that you will have to go several times even after that before she finally settles down. You might be doing the same thing for the next several nights, too.

A Process, Not a Recipe

Let's not pretend that sleep training is easy. Some babies get very upset when they are left to cry, even for three minutes. But we don't know until we try. My three-minute method isn't a recipe that everyone uses in the same way. It's an attitude and a strategy for approaching sleep difficulties that isn't too hard on Mom or baby, because the crying lasts only a short time.

If your baby has a very strong reaction when you try to change a bad sleeping pattern, he'll let you know. It might be difficult for you to calm him down. In that case, you need to have a plan B. For example, if you have to go in and out of the room, and the whole process lasts for more than an hour, it's probably best to feed him, even though that's what you're trying to change. Remember that crying makes a baby hungry and thirsty. And I have to add, sometimes you also have to make your own life easier. Without a feeding, your baby will cry for a longer time. One more feeding will help both of you get to sleep faster. After all, this little one has been fed during the night since he was born. Sometimes we have to be flexible. The next night, he might not wake up at all. But if he does, wait three minutes, go into his room, comfort him, and start the whole process again.

Remember, you are working toward something here. Your baby is not going to miraculously change habits overnight. So while you want your baby to sleep better, you also want this to happen without hard crying. Every baby is different. How long it takes to disrupt an old pattern depends on how old your baby is, her temperament, what you've done so far, and what you're trying to change. For example, if you are using the three-minute method to lengthen your child's naps, your goal is to break a too-short-sleep habit. Little by little, you use the three minutes to coax her back to sleep and to extend her naptime. But if you're also cutting out a feeding, you are trying to change two habits: the feeding itself and the sleep period.

Kindness First, Habit Later

With Oliver, we had all agreed: it was time to take away that three A.M. feeding, and we needed to teach him how to sleep through the night. To keep his tummy full, we would still give him the eleven P.M. feeding. Our ultimate goal was no food in the middle of the night, but we also had to give his body a chance to adjust to not having food at that hour. We knew he wasn't hungry at three A.M. and that he didn't need the extra nutrition, but he was used to it. It was kinder to wean him gradually—give him some food at first, but every night give him less. Once we cut down his food to almost nothing, then we could use the three-minute method to help him learn how to get back to sleep without it.

Gradually weaning a baby from a nighttime feeding is easier if he takes it in a bottle, as Oliver did. For months, I had been giving him his mother's pumped breast milk at night. I could see exactly how much he was consuming, and once we decided to wean him from it, I could easily pour one half-ounce less into the bottle for his three A.M. feeding.

It's a little trickier if your baby is breast-fed in the middle of the night, because you can't see how much she takes in. In that case, cut down on the feeding time by 15 percent. For example, you'd go from a normal twenty-minute feeding to seventeen minutes. If your baby's night feeding is already short—say, ten minutes, use the same 15 percent idea, and shorten the duration of the feeding by one or two minutes.

Don't worry, Mom, cutting down this way won't cause your body to produce less milk. As I explained earlier, you produce less milk at the end of the day anyway. As long as your baby is feeding well during the day, your body will continue to manufacture what she needs.

With breast or bottle, stay at each new level for three days. Then cut down again, on either quantity or time. Keep doing it until you're almost not feeding at all during the night. If she's still waking up and asking for it, use the three-minute method.

When Oliver got down to just one ounce, he continued to wake up at three A.M., but I knew that by then, his body had adjusted to having less milk, and his need for nutrition was gone. When he protested—remember, he was still in the habit of waking up at that hour—we let him cry for three minutes at a time. He was almost a year old when the pattern changed completely, and he slept through the night.

TO CHANGE OR NOT TO CHANGE?

A word about diapers: If your baby has been getting a full feeding, you might be in the habit of changing her diaper in the middle of the night, too. When you first begin to reduce the amount of food you give her, you will have to change her. Otherwise, she might wake early because of a soaking-wet diaper. Be patient. Subtract a half-ounce, or nurse for two or three minutes less each night. The less she drinks, the lighter her diaper. Eventually, you'll be able to stop changing her.

I also recommend buying overnight diapers, because they hold in the moisture and are less prone to leaking, which increases the chances that her peeing won't wake her. And if you're wondering about poop in the middle of the night, it usually doesn't happen. But if it does, of course you have to change your baby. Just don't make it a social event.

Keep At It

The three-minute method works pretty much the same way for all sleep-related issues: cutting out a night feeding, helping your baby go to sleep on his own, discouraging early wake-ups, extending naps. It's always a similar process. Perform the sleep ritual as usual, put him into his crib, say good night, and leave the room. He might protest. Wait the three minutes. Comfort him if necessary. Once you start, though, please stay the course. Your baby needs opportunities to soothe himself. He also might have to *relearn*. I've seen "good sleepers" mysteriously start waking again. Often, it's because something throws off her routine, such as a cold or teething. The three-minute method can help her get back on track. You also might need the three-minute method again when your baby is a little older and separation anxiety sets in. You might be upset that you're having to do this again. But each time, it will feel a little more familiar.

One word of caution. Because I work with babies every day, I can promise you that sometimes, no matter what you do, your baby will refuse to go back to sleep. This is perfectly normal. You'll probably have to hold him until he falls back to sleep or deal with his crankiness for the rest of the day. On those days, just know that you can try again tomorrow.

My three-minute method is not harsh. Think of it as another "classroom," an arena in which you provide guidance for your precious little one. If you consistently give her the opportunity to learn, she will find her pacifier or her "blanky" or some other object that comforts her. Or she will stare at something in the room that distracts her. She will calm herself, and that will reinforce the lesson.

And while you're getting there, don't forget to have compassion for your baby. Most adults do not like to sleep alone, either, or, for that matter, to be told they have to take a different route when they're used to going their own way. Every human must learn to adapt, including our babies. So let's train them without trying to control them. Be firm when you need to be, and be flexible when you can. In the end, your baby will see that his crib is safe and trust that you are close by when he needs help. And he will know how to go back to sleep on his own.

Oliver became so content in his bed that even when he was fighting a cold, he liked to lie in his crib. Not all babies react the same way. However, I believe that one reason for our success with Oliver was that even before we tried to wean him from the night feeding, he knew what to expect: eat, play, sleep. A baby with a good routine learns to sleep through the night faster than a baby whose days are unpredictable.

Oliver already had self-soothing tools that he could reach for. He also had more control over his body than a younger baby and could reach and grab anything he wanted. So every now and then, when he woke up in the middle of the night, he'd look for his pacifier, clutch his little white lamb for comfort, and put himself back to sleep. Some nights, he stood up in his crib and cried for a minute or two. But then he'd turn on his aquarium and distract himself. In a few minutes, he'd sit down, reach for his sleep buddies, and lie quietly until he drifted off to sleep. Life got a lot better for everyone.

Chapter 20

YOUR BABY OR YOUR BOSS?

As I came to writing the end of this book about your baby's beginning, I realized I wanted to leave you with some thoughts that will help you look toward the future. What kind of child your baby becomes has a lot to do with how you handle her now. I believe in looking ahead and stopping problems before they become too stubborn. As a caretaker of our most precious resource—people—I believe we show our love to these little sweet beings by paying attention to them, taking action and making changes when necessary, and anticipating what might come next.

By putting your baby on a dependable routine, you are making sure that her basic needs are being met. And by training her to soothe herself on awakening, to amuse herself at times throughout the day, and to sleep on her own, you are nudging her toward independence and teaching her valuable lessons in self-control.

How Baby Becomes Boss

Some parents start down a wrong road and keep taking it, and instead of helping their babies develop self-control, they put their *baby* in control. Some parents don't know another way. Others search frantically for advice, get confused, and then do whatever seems easiest at the time—holding the baby for hours, Mom using herself as a pacifier, Dad driving the baby around at midnight just to quiet him down. Then they try to get "tough." They let the baby "cry it out" and almost immediately feel guilty. So they go back to the constant comforting. There's no happy middle.

Believe me, I know that caring for an infant is not easy. I know that it's really difficult to let your baby cry for even three minutes. It takes strength and determination to change bad habits, and I understand that can be hard. But if you take what seems like the easy road, your baby might soon become your boss.

Let me tell you about Amelia, whom I first met in the park when she was three. She was being cared for by Theresa, a colleague of mine. Normally, my friend worked at night for the family, but on this particular morning, her daytime replacement was ill, so Theresa had to take a double shift. I was shocked that a child of Amelia's age still woke up several times a night and needed an adult's help, but once I heard the whole story, I knew why.

Amelia had been a difficult-to-calm baby, who cried and cried much of the day and night during her first three months. The pediatrician called her "colicky" and told her parents, Dave and Monique, that they just had to ride it out. In three or four months, he claimed, Amelia would "get over it."

Monique was close to forty when she had Amelia and had waited a long time to be a mother. She had read many baby books. Even though she had professional help from the day Amelia arrived, Monique had very definite ideas about child-rearing and wanted things done *her* way. She instructed the baby nurse to hold Amelia all the time and to do whatever it took to calm her and keep her from crying. As it turned out, the "trick" that worked best was for Mom, Dad, or (most often) the baby nurse to hold Amelia and bounce on a large vinyl exercise ball for at least fifteen minutes, a long and unpleasant time for the adult. It wasn't too safe, either. Imagine if one slipped off the ball!

Four months and two baby nurses later, just as the pediatrician predicted, Amelia's "colic" was gone. But by then, her bad habits were there to stay. During the day, because the parents couldn't bear to hear their baby cry, her desires were met on the spot. No one said no to Amelia. At night, she still needed an adult's help to fall asleep. The next nanny, who was a bit older than her predecessors, refused to use the exercise ball. Still, to keep the parents happy and to keep Amelia from crying, she walked around the room for hours at night, vigorously bouncing the little girl in her arms.

So what is Amelia like at age three? She still hasn't learned to sleep on her own. She is now too old to bounce. Theresa, who took over when the older nanny quit, also sleeps in Amelia's room. Every night, she has to get into bed *with* Amelia and hold her hand until she falls asleep. When that doesn't work, she spoons Amelia, hugging her tightly until she finally drifts off. And if Amelia wakes up in the middle of the night, Theresa is there to help her get back to sleep.

But the problem is no longer just about sleep. Amelia never learned to amuse or soothe herself. Now, as a preschooler, she's having a hard time of it. She lacks basic social skills. She's impolite. And having never learned the meaning of the word "no," she whines or has a tantrum whenever she doesn't get her own way.

Amelia's parents adore her and are willing to tolerate her behavior. They jokingly refer to her as "the boss" and think she's "cute" and "spunky." Others in the household, such as Theresa, have to take it, because the parents are paying them to do what Amelia wants. But outside the protected environment of her home, at preschool and at the park, Amelia encounters adults and children who don't have to play by her rules. When she grabs toys or stamps her feet because another child doesn't want to do what she wants, the adults roll their eyes, and the children walk away.

Of course, most three-year-olds still don't like to share, but they learn . . . as long as someone teaches them. I feel sorry for Amelia. She doesn't understand why other children don't want to play with her. When I witnessed such a scene at the park with my friend, the expression on Amelia's face said, *How dare they leave? I still want to play!*

The Problem with Baby Bosses

I worry about how a child like Amelia will be able to withstand life's challenges if she can't master basic emotional skills. Theresa didn't feel it was her place to suggest to the parents that Amelia had a problem. I find myself sometimes walking that narrow line with my clients, too. If Amelia had been in my care, her parents might not have listened to my advice. But I would have at least tried to explain that giving in to a child is not the same as comforting her. I would have encouraged them to reinforce Amelia's independence, rather than training her to rely on adults for entertainment and soothing. I would have stressed that when we deprive a child of opportunities to wait, to calm herself, and to spend time on her own, there's a good chance that she will become a toddler who whines, who has tantrums, and whom no one wants to be around. I want the best for the babies I care for. I want them to be strong and self-sufficient, because life always presents new challenges.

By the way, I also worry about the parents in these cases. A few years after they married, a couple I knew decided to adopt. They were lovely people, the mother a teacher, the father a business-man. First they adopted a baby girl and then a baby boy. I later learned that they had divorced. I found out why when I ran into the father at the supermarket. By then, he'd remarried and started another family.

"Luiza, my marriage started to fall apart when my children took over," he explained. "Our household was chaotic. Nine years later, we split up."

It was a sadly familiar story. Neither of the parents had a plan for adding kids to their life. The babies arrived, and a few months later, the mother went back to work. There was no predictable routine. The mother took care of things as they came up. The father loved to do "fun" things with the kids, but he let his wife do most of the hands-on care, the training of the nanny, and whatever else was needed to make the household run.

The children had no discipline, no rules to guide them. They got more and more confused and, of course, became increasingly difficult to deal with. The mother felt guilty for leaving the house every day, so whenever she was at home, she spent every moment catering to the children, which left no time for herself or for her marriage. The children had no boundaries, so she had two little bosses. I am not saying that the children were the ones to be blamed, nor were the mother or father, for that matter. But an entire family can spin out of control when children are allowed to take over.

A New Way to Think About Discipline

If you're still dealing with an infant issue, such as feeding or sleeping, you probably haven't thought much about discipline. You might be wondering, *Isn't she getting ahead of herself? Isn't this a handbook about babies?*

But without your even realizing it, in small, everyday ways, you are already teaching your child discipline by helping her develop emotionally. When you stick to your routine, make her wait, talk to her, and set limits, you are helping her learn how to deal with her environment. You're teaching her the rules. Let's review the main strands of advice I offer in this book with discipline in mind. Each suggestion came from years of watching babies with their mothers. The first two you will find familiar, so I don't need to explain them. If you've read and followed the advice in this book, you're probably already practicing them. All of the advice is designed to build your child's confidence and emotional skills, which will make both of your lives easier down the road a bit.

Take time to bond with your baby. Love and affection between mother and child (or between child and whoever regularly takes care of him) provide a foundation on which trust is built. Remember that I told Oliver's parents he was more likely to respond to my doing the three-minute method instead of a new nanny, a stranger? He already trusted me. When you bond with your baby, it becomes easy to guide him toward the road you believe is best. Children love to please the people they love.

Establish a regular but flexible routine. Eat, play, sleep. When life is predictable, even difficult-to-calm babies feel more secure. They know what's coming next, and their needs are met in a timely manner. Life doesn't hit them with surprises. These babies are more relaxed and less prone to emotional outbursts.

Nudge your baby toward independence. Don't laugh—there is such a thing as an "independent baby"—and I've been helping you lay the groundwork since day one. Your little one is not ready for school just yet. But independence now means that she can already soothe herself on waking, amuse herself throughout the day, and put herself to sleep. She has started to master emotional skills that will grow with her. An independent baby is easier to distract and to discipline than a child raised in chaos.

Teach your baby to wait. Always look for ways to hit "pause" before you respond to your baby. One of the benefits of my three-minute method is that it teaches your baby to wait. As your baby gets older and has learned to wait, can play on his own, and goes to sleep easily, those early roots of self-control will give him tools to face new challenges and to "manage" his emotional self. He might not like to hear "no"—what toddler does? Still, he probably won't have an oversized reaction to it, such as a tantrum. When he picks up a precious vase from your coffee table, you can more easily distract him. You might say, "Wait, look at this," and then show him something he's allowed to handle.

Talk to your baby constantly. Babies who are talked to are babies who know how to relate to people. Talking can take several forms. Report what you're doing ("We're going for a walk"). Notice and name objects for your baby ("Look at the doggie"). Sing songs. Read him books. Remember, too, that talking isn't just about acquiring language. It also teaches values. Talking "civilizes" children by letting them know what you (and society) expect from them. We let them know what a "nice" person does by acting kindly and respectfully toward them. We teach them to say please and thank you, even before they have the words for it. We show them how not to interrupt ("One second, Matthew, Sally and I are talking"). And we model good conversation for them. Eventually, they become polite, respectful children, who know to shake hands and look people in the eye.

Satisfy your baby's curiosity, and also set limits. Earlier, we talked about limiting your child's physical space by putting fragile and dangerous objects out of reach. But remember that you're dealing with a little scientist. When he points to Aunt Tillie's precious vase on a high shelf, take it down for a moment. Satisfy his curiosity by letting him touch it. (This is a good time to say, "Be gentle," a phrase you'll probably repeat when he's with other children or pets!) He will see that it's hard, that it has a pretty pattern. Then put it back.

It's also important for you to start to limit your child's actions so that he learns to avoid danger and respond to directions when he's headed toward it. We want to teach children to "use their words," right? Well, here we need to remember to use *our* words, too. This is exceptionally important once your baby starts to move and can somehow go from where you've placed him to where he wants to be. Words teach him, limit him, and warn him.

Use short phrases, and be careful not to use words that will confuse him. For example, consider the word "touch." It's not a good idea to use a phrase such as "Don't touch that wire," because touching is how your baby learns. And he might not yet have learned what a "wire" is. Besides, while you're trying to say, "I'm afraid you're going to get hurt," or "I'm worried that you'll break that," what you *mean* to say is, "No!" So use the name of the object ("vase") he is trying to touch with the word "no," as in "No vase." Or just look him in the eye and say, "No, no!"

At first, he probably won't understand—or listen. Be firm but gentle with your command, and then redirect him to a safer place to give him another object that he *can* touch, such as a toy or a plastic container. Distracting him and changing his focus away from the wire or the vase is a double win: the child learns words *and* restraint. He's learning the rules.

It's Worth It, and It Works (Eventually)

I sometimes have to hold my tongue when I visit families. No matter how good their intentions, I see two typical scenarios that seem to confuse their children rather than discipline them:

> ▸ The parents baby-proof the house but, at the same time, decide not to move any of their possessions out of their little explorer's reach. Now everything their baby touches gets a big loud "No!" I'm not sure he learns anything from that kind of experience, except that everything is off limits. And the word "no" loses its meaning.

› The parents use physical discipline—a spanking or a slap on the hand. They *then* redirect their child to something or someplace that's acceptable. The problem with this approach is that the child learns that when he wants to interact with his environment, he gets hurt. Even worse, he has had to endure the upset and the pain of being physically harmed. Those bad feelings linger, even if the parents distract him by giving him a toy or carrying him to a safer place.

I would not recommend either of these strategies, because they are unkind. They either confuse your baby or make him feel bad. And they teach nothing. Your baby's brain is developing quickly, as are his motor skills. At birth, he was a blank slate, but now he is taking it all in—the good and the bad. He will gain knowledge through experience.

If you must "discipline" your baby—that is, show her a better way to act—do it with love in your heart. Let her know that something (or someplace) is off limits or that certain behavior is not allowed. There is a wrong and a right. And this is the right way to teach your child limitations and, eventually, the difference between right and wrong.

Mom, take several deep breaths. Understand that when it comes to setting limits, you will have to repeat yourself over and over and over and over until you sound like a recording. But that little empty infant brain will fill and grow. Be gentle, be very consistent and patient, and require that everyone who cares for your young scientist-explorer does the same.

It will be worth it, because you'll have a baby, not a boss.

NOTES ON THE
THIRD MONTH AND BEYOND

Your baby will keep changing and growing in amazing ways. Here's a handy way to keep track over the next few months.

Third Month

Weight: _____

Height:_____

Firsts and other milestones:_____

_____

_____

Favorite toys/activities: _____

_____

_____

How has the eat-play-sleep routine changed? _____

_____

_____

What else is new or different? _____

_____

_____

_____

Sixth Month

Weight: _____

Height:_____

Firsts and other milestones:_____

_____

_____

_____

Favorite toys/activities: _____

_____

_____

_____

How has the eat-play-sleep routine changed? _____

_____

_____

_____

What else is new or different? _____

_____

_____

_____

_____

_____

_____

Ninth Month and Beyond

Weight: _____

Height:_____

Firsts and other milestones:_____

_____

_____

_____

Favorite toys/activities: _____

_____

_____

_____

How has the eat-play-sleep routine changed? _____

_____

_____

_____

What else is new or different? _____

_____

_____

_____

_____

_____

_____

Epilogue

HOW IMPORTANT *YOU* ARE!

At the end of the day, who your baby is now and who she will turn out to be is out of your control and mine. How a baby becomes a person is still a mystery. All we know is that nature and nurture both play a part and affect each other. Is either more powerful?

No one knows. Children "come in" with their own biology and a genetic code that partly determines who they are. Some are more stubborn or more sensitive. But I don't believe that any of them are "terrible." Even the easiest baby can be affected by poor childcare. So while nature influences your baby, her environment also plays a part—in my opinion, the bigger part.

I wouldn't be as passionate about my role as a baby nurse if I didn't believe that constant care and love always help shape a child's behavior and attitudes for the better. Your baby is learning even when you're not teaching her.

We are what we have learned and experienced in our formative years, starting when we are still in our cribs. When I work with a child for more than one year, he understands Portuguese, because that's how I communicate with the babies in my charge. He starts to like some of my music and my food. When you "mother" a child, you share yourself, and he takes you in.

How do I know that nurture means so much? It's not just because I have had the privilege to usher so many babies through their first three months or because the children under my care learn to like parts of my culture. It's not just because I have seen firsthand what a difference a positive, confident mom makes even with a difficult-to-calm baby. It is also because I recognize how the power of nurturing shaped me.

My morals, values, and much of what I am today I learned from my mother in my early years. Even though I emigrated from my country when I was only twenty-seven years old, the base I still stand on today is one my mother built for me in Brazil. My mother and her circle of women in our village—the young mothers who turned to her for advice and comfort—are with me every day.

My point is that we shape babies' lives, with our touch and our love, with our words and our deeds, just as we have been shaped by our mothers. We women are the teachers. When our babies are young, we have the power to shape those tiny creatures into good human beings. So do fathers, of course (as well as others who take care of him). But as I said at the beginning of this book, even as Dad takes a greater role in nurturing, women are the mainstay. So let's use this power with pride and consciousness. In the end, there is no more important job.

Mom, if you're reading this book, it means that you are only at the starting line, taking small steps toward the future that will shape your baby's behavior. Everything you do in the eat, play, sleep cycle opens the world to him. You'll get more out of the experience of mothering if you worry less about what he will *be* and, instead, appreciate how he is *now*. Soak up his cooing and his smiles. Watch how he suddenly notices the dog or realizes that when he arches his back and turns his neck, he rolls over. This is a time of amazing accomplishments. In each moment, a miracle is taking place. Your baby is learning to connect, to think, and to experiment with new sounds and motions.

You might not believe me. Maybe you had a rough start and are still dealing with sleepless nights and a lot of crying. Or perhaps you got off to a good start and now face an unexpected challenge. Either way, take a deep breath. This time will pass. You can do it. There's also a surprise bonus: being attentive, patient, and open, reminding yourself how important you are, and handling whatever comes your way will make you feel good about yourself and make you an even better mother. You gain confidence from knowing that even if there's no end in sight and no obvious solution, you can get through it.

One of the books I love to read to "my" babies is *The Carrot Seed* by Ruth Krauss. I like it because it has few words and simple pictures. But it also has a great message and not just for children. It's for you, too. The book begins:

A little boy planted a carrot seed.

His mother said, "I'm afraid it won't come up."

Everyone—his father and his big brother—feels pretty much the same way about the boy's project. But the little boy doesn't get discouraged. He keeps weeding and watering the plant. For many pages, we see that no carrot grows in the spot where he planted the seed. Everyone keeps saying it won't come up. But the boy persists, every day pulling up weeds and watering the ground around it.

And then, one day, a carrot came up

just as the little boy had known it would.

And on the last page, we see the little boy carting a giant carrot in his wheelbarrow, presumably on the way home to show his family.

OK, Mom, I know you're not trying to raise a carrot, but caring for a new baby requires the same mix of effort, time, and faith. Stick with your routine and with the practices you believe in. Others might say to you, "That will never work." But their opinions won't matter if you trust yourself and know your baby.

Acknowledgments

From its original conception to the final manuscript, *Eat, Play, Sleep* has been in the making for more than fifteen years. But it was in the last three years that this book truly became a reality. I have many people to thank.

My lifelong friend in Brazil, Professor Dr. Luiz Octávio Lima Camargo inspired me to think about my philosophy of baby care and suggested that I write it all down.

Hope Angnelli, asking nothing in return, kindly edited the first rough. My friends Marcia Melo and Jerome Stasny helped with the translation when the early manuscript was still in Portuguese.

My dear friend Inge Lopes's expertise in biology helped me to understand the effects of nutrition and medications on tiny baby bodies.

My long-term baby-nurse partner, Jane Lopes, took over for me on my days off. She bolstered my spirit when I didn't believe I was capable of this huge challenge and kept encouraging me when it all seemed too hard.

Cindy Crawford patiently read the first drafts of this book, gave me valuable input and, later, kindly agreed to write the Foreword.

Leslie Moonves and his wife, Julie Chen, gave me the gift of believing in my work. They told others about me and put the manuscript in the right hands.

I also wish to thank Dana Walden for her ongoing support and for introducing me to Ryan Murphy and David Miller.

I am grateful to all my clients. They have welcomed me into their homes, trusted me with their babies, and made me a part of their families. It is their stories that give life to my work.

Melinda Blau helped me crystallize my knowledge and experience and gave this book its unique step-by-step form.

Greer Hendricks, my editor, along with her team at Simon & Schuster, went beyond the call of duty to turn this manuscript into a beautiful book.

Finally, I thank my mother, who is with me in memory. She gave me a solid foundation and an understanding of babies that I always carry with me. It is to her that I owe my deepest appreciation.

—*Luiza DeSouza*
Beverly Hills, California

Index